The NEW RtI:

Response to Intelligence

Updated 2nd Edition

Penny Choice, M.A., M.Ed.
Sally Walker, Ph.D.

Kathy Balsamo, Editor

D1097055

Pieces of Learning

The NEW RtI: Response to Intelligence

2010 Texas Legacy Award Winner
for Educators

CLC0473
© 2011 Pieces of Learning
Marion IL
ISBN 978-1-934358-91-7
Printed by McNaughton & Gunn, Inc
Saline MI USA
06/2011

"For Gifted Children everywhere:

May they receive the education they so desperately need."

Acknowledgements

Penny would like to thank the Regional Office of Education in Lake County, IL: Roycealee J. Wood, Superintendent of Schools, in her ongoing commitment to supporting gifted children and their education; Tim Yoder, Media Specialist, who provided the techie support in creating the model design online; and Jennie Winters, Math/Science Coordinator for her excellent contribution of the math intervention section.

Penny is eternally grateful to Dr. Sally Walker, Executive Director for the Illinois Association for Gifted Children for being a mentor extraordinaire, and to the many professionals in Gifted Education who have been there for her over and over again.

She would also like to thank editor, Kathy Balsamo, for her invaluable assistance and support.

Thanks also to Ian, Haley, Braden, and Taryn. Hopefully this book will have a positive impact on their education.

Sally thanks the Board of Directors and Committee Chairs of the Illinois Association for Gifted Children, both past and present, for their dedication and commitment to gifted children. Their leadership in the state has kept gifted education alive.

To Trent, Taylor, Harrison and Ellary, may you benefit from the educational foundation that has been laid.

Table of Contents

Preface

Education is changing radically in its attempt to meet the demands of the 21st Century global economy. As we move from a public school system created to meet the needs of the Industrial Age to one designed for the Post Information Age (also called the Conceptual Age), the shift to creating appropriate education for ALL students becomes essential. Unfortunately, in public education, this has come to mean helping struggling students be successful in classrooms across the country–often at the expense of students who can easily master the age-level curriculum.

How did this happen?

It began with the 1983 report for educational reform known as *A Nation at Risk* where it was discovered that many students in classrooms across the United States were not learning and growing enough to prepare them for the world in which they were going to live. Then came the No Child Left Behind Act (NCLB, 2001) a punitive law that required all students to pass a yearly, high-stakes, state-determined test in reading and math. Schools who did not meet the federal requirements for passing the test (which, by the way, increased every year to the goal of 100% by 2014) were punished with sanctions. This put schools in fear of restrictions that would affect their federal funding, and that often led to the instructional charge to *teach to the test.* The focus again shifted to struggling students and often left high-average and gifted students behind.

But it remained that many students could not achieve the minimum competency levels required to pass the state test. They needed more intervention in order to meet federal guidelines.

In 2004, it was decided to include support for these students in the initiative named Response to Intervention (For the purpose of clarity, Response to Intervention is referred to as RtI) under the reauthorization of the Individuals with Disabilities

Education Act (IDEA, 2004). The purpose of RtI began as a general education initiative. It was quickly adapted by the Division for Learning Disabilities of the Council for Exceptional Children (CEC) in 2007, to support the special education law by promoting evidence-based instruction in classrooms and to help general, remedial, and special education work together. Districts scrambled in order to meet the new guidelines. In Illinois, for example, districts were required by the Illinois State Board of Education (ISBE) in Illinois Rules (2008), to submit a plan for meeting these guidelines by January, 2009.

According to CEC, the purpose of RtI is threefold:

1. research-based implementation in general education of instruction and interventions,
2. assessment of students of these interventions, and
3. use of assessment data for decision-making.

Once again, high-ability students could be left behind.

It seems as if there is always an up-and-coming initiative that proposes to close the achievement gap. Closing the achievement gap is usually interpreted as bringing up lower scores to be closer to the higher ones. Currently, the newest educational initiative called the *Race to the Top* provides competitive grants to districts that raise student achievement through implementation of the American Recovery and Reinvestment Act of 2009 (ARRA). Whether this act will ultimately benefit gifted learners remains to be seen. Unfortunately, the focus still appears to be on high-stakes testing for minimum competency and **not** for individual growth and challenge.

Will high-ability students be left behind again?

Evidence continues to accumulate supporting the loss of educational opportunity for high-end students. A study by the Center for Evaluation and Education Policy at Indiana University, Bloomington, IN, indicates that the emphasis on bringing struggling students' scores up on high-stakes testing is affecting the growth of students at the high end (Plucker, Burroughs, & Song, 2010).The focus of current testing is for minimum competency instead of for excellence (Plucker et al., 2010).

A report titled *State of the States in Gifted Education* (National Association for Gifted Children [NAGC], 2009b) found that gifted children continue to be ignored in the United States. According to the report "there is a markedly insufficient national commitment to gifted and talented children, which, if left unchecked, will ultimately leave our nation unprepared to field the next generation of innovators and to compete in the global economy" (NAGC, 2009b, p. 2).

The data in this report states that:

- there is little support for funding,
- teachers are unprepared to meet gifted student needs,
- services for gifted children are very inconsistent, and
- there is a lack of accountability and reporting to support services.

There are over three million gifted and talented students in the United States, representing diverse experiences, expertise, and cultural backgrounds, who deserve an appropriate educational system to help them achieve their highest potential.

As a call to action, The Executive Summary of the *State of the States in Gifted Education* report states, "As high-ability learners sit bored in classrooms around the country, our nation is failing to meet their learning, social, and emotional needs that are key to their success" (NAGC, 2009b, p. 4).

In 2009, NAGC issued a position statement calling for the addition of interventions for gifted learners into the RtI framework (NAGC, 2009a). It addresses screening and assessment, establishing protocols, and the provisions of tiered supports and services to meet the needs of gifted students. It also addresses the importance of meeting the needs of twice-exceptional students through RtI.

RtI continues to guide all public education with its focus on struggling students. So what does this mean for gifted and talented students and THEIR education?

REFERENCES

American Recovery and Reinvestment Act of 2009. Public Law 111-5.

Division for Learning Disabilities of the Council for Exceptional Children (2007). Reston, VA: Author.

Individuals with Disabilities Education Improvement Act, Pub. Law 108-446 (December 3, 2004).

Illinois State Board of Education, (2008). Illinois Rules. Springfield, IL: Author.

Plucker, J. A., Burroughs, N., & Song, R. (2010). *Mind the (other) gap! The growing excellence gap in K–12 education.* Bloomington, IN: Center for Evaluation and Education Policy.

National Association for Gifted Children. (2009a). *Response to intervention for gifted children.* Retrieved from http://www.nagc.org/index.aspx?id=6266

National Association for Gifted Children (2009b). *State of the states in gifted education:* 2008-2009. Washington, D.C.: Author.

National Commission on Excellence in Education. (1983). *A nation at risk: The imperative for educational reform.* Washington, DC: U.S. Government Printing Office.

No Child Left Behind Act, PL 107-110, (2001).

WEBSITES

www.ed.gov:	U.S. Department of Education Homepage
www.ed.gov/nclb/landing.jhtml:	No Child Left Behind
www.rti4success.org:	National Center on Response to Intervention
www.dldcec.org:	Division for Learning Disabilities of the Council for Exceptional Children

Elements of
Response to Intervention (RtI)

What does RtI mean for gifted students–What can be done about this current educational initiative and its impact on gifted education? What can we do to integrate RtI into curriculum for gifted and talented learners? What can be done to assure that all students are learning all that they can? How can we prevent the gifted from being left behind . . . again?

We begin by looking at the structure of RtI.

RtI was created to raise student achievement through a tiered model of intervention beginning with services in reading. It has come to include other content areas (usually math). It began with a desire to help students in the early grades but now has been stretched to middle and high school classrooms. Its objective is to modify teacher lesson plans based on frequent monitoring of progress. It was created as a general education initiative for all students, but it has evolved to meet the needs of struggling students who are having difficulty being successful in the regular education classroom. These students in the regular classroom were unable to pass the high-stakes state test, yet they did not qualify for special education services. As a result, districts received lower scores on state high-stakes tests resulting in punitive action for the district. RtI became the mechanism to support districts and to raise test scores. Some states have even made the use of RtI a requirement for funding. In many states, RtI takes on the following format (Figure 1.1):

Tier 1 is the foundation or the core curriculum (grade level) designed for ALL students. The majority of students–80-85%–are learning and growing in a grade-level curriculum.

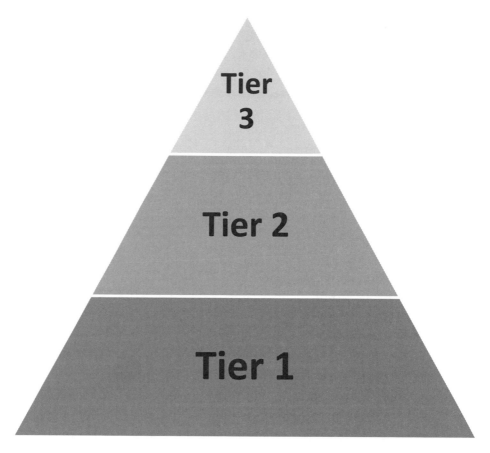

Figure 1.1. Response to Intervention Model.

Tier 2 includes **supplemental instruction and intervention** in ADDITION to the core curriculum instruction.

Tier 3 consists of **intensive instructional interventions** in ADDITION to the core instruction. Students are identified for Tiers 2 and 3 through ongoing assessment. Data-based decision making is applied across the tiers.

How does this design impact gifted students? The majority of students (80–85%) are assumed to be successful in Tier 1. **Does this seem to be a return to the *one size fits all* approach to education?** Tier 1 assumes that most students need the same curriculum and instruction that is appropriate only for those students who can master the curriculum with teacher support. Many gifted students master the grade-level curriculum very quickly. Although figures differ, up to 50% or more of gifted students have mastered the age-level curriculum before they enter the classroom at the beginning of the year (Reis, Burns, & Renzulli, 1992). These students with one or two exposures often master the remaining curriculum. The implication is that many gifted students are frustrated, waiting to learn something new in the classroom for the majority of every school day.

Differentiation Is Not Guaranteed

Another assumption of RtI is that differentiated instructional practices are taking place in ALL classrooms. This means that classroom teachers are differentiating their instruction to provide multiple opportunities at various levels of learning. It is assumed also that differentiated instructional strategies are being provided for ALL learners, providing them with scientific research-based interventions.

Those strategies for gifted and talented students include active engagement, choice, compacting, extensions, flexible grouping, higher level thinking skills, independent study, learning centers, learning contracts, open-ended assignments, RAFT assignments, and tiered lessons.

Staff developers who have offered professional development in differentiation have found that, in fact, differentiation is very difficult to implement in the classroom. Teachers find it challenging to provide differentiation when they have up to 30 or more students in their classrooms and must simultaneously attempt to teach the regular curriculum **and** assess all students for readiness. Providing differentiation for students who have already mastered the content becomes a daunting task. Yet states suggest that differentiated practices take place in all classes.

Teachers have said that differentiation may take place less than 10% of the time they teach (P. Choice, personal communication, 1995; Gavin & Adelson, 2008;

Tomlinson, 2003). Dr. Carol Ann Tomlinson (2003), well known in the field of diffe-rentiation, has said that teachers seldom differentiate in classrooms and less often for exceptionalities. Colleges and universities provide sporadic coursework in diffe-rentiation both at the undergraduate and graduate levels. The result is that differen-tiation is randomly taking place in the classroom at any grade level or in any content area.

Assessment of Gifted Students

A brief mention of assessment that drives the RtI model: Assessment is essential, and RtI or any educational initiative must be data driven (Coil, 2009). However, one must be very careful about choosing assessments to determine intervention for gifted students. Many assessments are measures of minimum competency used to determine grade-level achievement. These assessments may demonstrate that the gifted student is at the top, but they do not show how much more the student knows. Special assessments are needed to go beyond the ceiling of grade-level competency. A district must work closely with gifted specialists to determine the val-ue of any assessment used with gifted students. Assessment forms specific to gifted students are on pages 55-62 (Coil, 2008).

The NEW RtI: Response to INTELLIGENCE Model™

How can educators fit gifted students into the RtI picture? Because gifted students have so many times been *left behind,* we must turn RtI, a Response to Intervention, into a **Response to INTELLIGENCE.**

Below are quotes regarding gifted education programs resulting from the struggle to implement Response to Intervention in their communities:

District superintendent: "We don't need our gifted program anymore because RtI will take care of gifted students' needs."

School principal: "Let's eliminate the gifted services because we need to concentrate on RtI."

Curriculum Director: "The state says we have to do RtI so that's just what we are going to do. Those gifted kids will do just fine."

Building Administrator: "We need to focus on struggling students so their test scores go up."

Teacher: "I can only find time to differentiate for some of my students. Struggling students can benefit the most. That's where RtI's focus is anyway."

The rumblings and ramblings in districts about the impact of Response to Intervention on gifted education continue. The emphasis continues to be on the struggling student and the achievement of minimum competency on high-stakes tests. What does this mean for gifted students?

A Workable Solution

This emphasis on struggling students and high-stakes test scores is clearly a problem for gifted students who learn early that school is easy, boring and, too often, not the place to be for real learning and growth.

But there IS a solution to this dilemma that will support students with high potential and give them the challenge and skills to be successful in their lives.

By modifying the three-tier triangular model, we can provide for ALL students. Tier 1 (all students) remains for the core, grade-level curriculum. But Tier 2 (small groups of at-risk students) and Tier 3 (intense individualized support) students can be found at **both** ends of the learning spectrum.

By turning the typical *Response to Intervention* model on its side and placing Tier 2 and Tier 3 students on a continuum, we can finally provide for ALL students in the classroom. This is at last, in Figure 1.2, a **Response to INTELLIGENCE.**

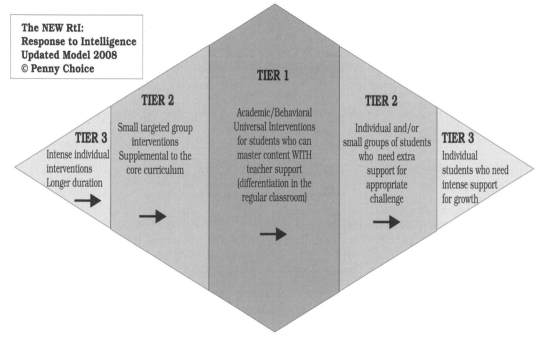

Figure 1.2. Response to Intelligence Model.

Objective for struggling students: *To be successful at Tier 1 or higher.*

Objective for advanced students: *To receive appropriate challenge for growth (and skill development) at least 1 year for every year spent in school.*

The left side of the continuum is for students who struggle with the regular curriculum. Interventions are provided for those students who need support in order to master the core curriculum. **Tier 1** (Figure 1.3) is for students who can master the content WITH teacher support.

On the right side of the continuum:

- **Tier 2** is for students who need extra support in order to be challenged appropriately and to develop the thinking skills needed for success in life; and
- **Tier 3** is for students who need intense support from a gifted education specialist (or the equivalent).

Tier 1

Differentiation is defined as: "the adaptation and modification of age-appropriate learning experiences in order to address the differences in student readiness levels, interests, and learning profiles" (Slade, 2002).

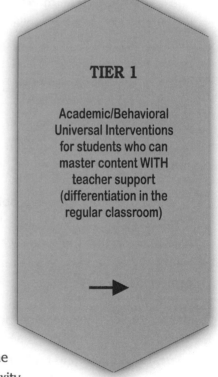

It is most appropriate when students need teacher support for mastery.

Teachers can differentiate the grade-level core curriculum by **altering the content, process,** or **product**.

Content can be altered by changing the pace, depth, and/or complexity of the material. To change the content, teachers may teach different or more difficult material. They may go deeper into the subject matter or cover the content in greater complexity.

Figure 1.3. Tier 1.

To change the **process**, teachers may go at a faster pace, use higher levels of thinking, or use different teaching strategies.

The purpose is to provide strategies that challenge high-end students and stretch their thinking at a more advanced level.

When teachers differentiate **product** they provide options for students to demonstrate mastery of the core curriculum content. Products can be written, verbal, visual, kinesthetic, or technological. They can range from a written report, an oral presentation, or a graphic organizer, to a play or video. This is the most commonly used differentiation in classrooms because many of the techniques are well known and easily applied.

One of the most often used strategies is tiered assignments where students create projects at different levels of readiness, interests, and learning profiles. Indiana's Tiered Curriculum Project is an excellent example of the use of tiering in reading, math, and science available through the internet. Other strategies include think-tac-toe, developed by Dr. Carol Ann Tomlinson, and the extension menu, created by Susan Winebrenner (2001). The strategy of RAFTing is also quite popular, where students create a project using different Roles, Audiences, Formats, and Topics. Excellent resources for tiering, think-tac-toes, and RAFTing incorporating readiness levels and learning profiles are *Demystifying Differentiation in Elementary School* (2008) and *Demystifying Differentiation in Middle School* (2007) by Caroline Eidson, Robert Iseminger, and Christopher Taibbi.

Many resources are available to teachers to develop their differentiation skills. (Resources are listed on page 131.) Parents must also become familiar with these resources so that they can recognize differentiated strategies that occur in classrooms. They can also guide teachers in the use of these strategies in the differentiated classroom.

Strategies necessary for the differentiated classroom are essential to successful Tier 1 support for students who are so different from each other in their readiness, interests, and learning profiles. Some gifted students can be supported quite well in classrooms committed to differentiation. It is important, however, that teachers use open-ended questioning, not *single, right-answer* thinking. Gifted kids often know the answer quickly and need questioning that encourages them to think. Thinking does not happen when one already knows the answer.

RtI assumes that differentiation is taking place in regular classrooms. Differentiation in the regular classroom is an appropriate Tier 1 strategy for some gifted students some of the time. How do we informally identify those gifted students who may need Tier 1 differentiation?

Teachers must ask three questions that will help them identify students who may require differentiation:

1. Who are the students who "get" the curriculum easily?
2. Do some students master the curriculum with one repetition–or know the material even before it is taught?
3. Do students sometimes become bored in the classroom, even demonstrating behavior problems?

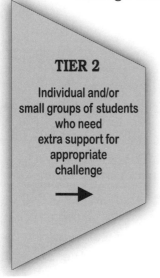

TIER 2

Individual and/or small groups of students who need extra support for appropriate challenge

Figure 1.4. Right Tier 2.

Right Tier 2

There are gifted students, however, that may qualify for Right Tiers 2 and 3 on the high end of the curriculum. These students may be at-risk if they do not receive appropriate support and opportunities for growth.

Figure 1.4 describes students who may qualify for Right Tier 2 (students who need targeted supplemental support in order to insure appropriate learning and growth). This Tier includes students who have been identified in standard areas of giftedness (as defined by many states):

- gifted in several/most content areas, sometimes called General Intellectual giftedness;
- gifted in one or more content areas, sometimes called Specific Academic giftedness; and
- students identified in other abilities: specific talent in music, art, writing, scientific thinking, leadership, etc.

Why do these students need Right Tier 2 support? Research has shown that if gifted students do not receive the appropriate amount of challenge above and beyond grade-level work, many of them learn to coast throughout their primary and secondary education (Rimm, 1997). This can lead to a lack of development of skills that all students need to be successful in their adult lives. These skills include, among others, problem-solving, critical and creative thinking, higher order thinking, risk-taking, sound reasoning, and the development of internal motivation and commitment to doing difficult work through struggle and challenge, resilience, persistence, and questioning.

Far too often bright students who do not have to work or struggle in school may find themselves in a challenging academic situation for the first time in college or beyond and do not have the skill set to be successful. Many college dropouts fit this description. Right Tier 2 support is invaluable in this situation.

Right Tier 2 interventions include:

- gifted services within the classroom with a gifted specialist;
- gifted services in resource rooms or replacement classes. Replacement classes group gifted students for reading, math, or other subjects for full daily instruction with a gifted specialist who uses compacting, acceleration, and enrichment of the curriculum in order to meet these students' needs. Replacement classes are classes that typically are held in a content area that is occurring at the same time in the regular classroom. Instead of completing the standard curriculum math, the replacement class focus may be on accelerated math content and skills. The replacement class meets daily, and the teacher of that class issues the homework and the grade for the content area;
- a continuum of services to meet individual students' needs; and
- any opportunity for gifted students to meet together in small groups.

Many students who have high potential may be seriously at risk of falling through the cracks in education. These students are often ignored in the public schools because it is very difficult to diagnose them correctly and even harder to serve them.

These students may need Right Tier 2 and Right Tier 3 interventions just as their struggling counterparts in education–and they need and deserve opportunities for diagnosis and support. One area of intense need for support includes those students who have dual/multiple exceptionalities. These students have been called *gifted and . . . (or) twice exceptional.*

Dual/multiple exceptionalities include:

- ADHD/ADD, etc.;
- visual/spatial learners;
- students with visual processing problems;
- Asperger's syndrome;
- physical impairment (e.g., hearing impaired);
- other learning differences: dysgraphia, dyslexia, dysphasia (linguistic function), dyscalculia, etc.; and
- English language learners.

Some of these students are identified for special education because their areas of need become evident. Frequently, however, their high potential is not diagnosed because of their more evident special needs.

There are also students equally as smart, yet they still have significant learning difficulties–and they often go unrecognized as needing support. They mask their deficiencies and seem average in learning potential. These students who may **look** like average students may be the most underserved and neglected. They know they are bright, and yet they have a learning problem that they carefully hide so no one discovers how bright they really are. These students definitely need Right Tier 2 interventions with targeted supplemental support. Some of these students need Right Tier 3 support that calls for individualized support to insure learning and growth at their levels of readiness.

Right Tier 3

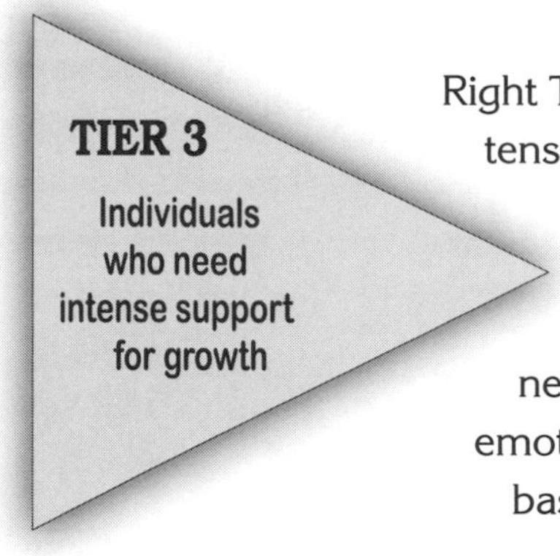

Right Tier 3 (Figure 1.5) describes students who need intense individual support in order to have their needs met. Some students are highly gifted, very different from other gifted students. They may have demonstrated a passion for learning in a given area and need support to grow. They may have significant social/emotional needs that could be supported on an individual basis. Whatever the need, support from a specialist is necessary for them to be learning and growing.

TIER 3

Individuals who need intense support for growth

Figure 1.5. Right Tier 3.

Many of these students will be on independent contracts. An example of a Right Tier 3 intervention involved a young lady who was in a sixth grade class that was beginning an overview of Ancient Greece. She had just finished reading *The Odyssey* by Homer and demonstrated mastery of the entire unit being studied. She developed an independent contract, created her own assessments, and did her extension unit that was at her level. Her work with the gifted specialist kept her focused.

Right Tier 3 students need intensive intervention as their needs vary greatly from their age-level peers. Gifted Tier 3 students require more than differentiation. In some cases, they need grade skipping, early admittance to middle school, high school, or college. Their intellectual abilities far surpass others their age. This knowledge is based on data and requires a team of knowledgeable professionals to make educational decisions that do not follow the norm.

Others Who May Need Right Tier 2 (Small Groups)
and Right Tier 3 (Intense Individual) Support

As our society becomes more diverse, we are beginning to recognize gifted students in those categories who need special services. The same percentage of these students have as high a potential as in the general student population (a minimum of 3-5% according to many state definitions). The following is a partial list describing other students who may need Right Tier 2 and Right Tier 3 support. They include:

- students dealing with poverty and homelessness,
- students who enter public education with limited life experiences,
- students identified as highly gifted (an IQ of over 150),
- students existentially gifted (highly sensitive, deep thinkers),
- rural gifted,
- creative gifted,
- culturally diverse/bilingual gifted,
- gifted students dealing with gender issues, and
- young gifted.

Differences Between Tier 2 and Tier 3 Support
on the Left (Struggling) and the Right (Advanced)

We cannot leave this chapter without noting that there is a significant difference between Tier 2 and Tier 3 on the struggling end of the continuum and of intervention and support at the gifted end of the continuum. Their purposes are entirely different, and the purpose of each is very important.

The objective for students on the struggling end (Left Tier 2 and Left Tier 3) is to process them as quickly as possible back into Tier 1. We want them to be as successful as possible with the grade-level core curriculum.

However, the objective for students at the higher end of the continuum is to move them into Tiers 2 and 3 as quickly as possible in order to provide them with optimum learning, growth, and curricular challenge.

This is an important concept and must be recognized in order to make the NEW RtI–Response to Intelligence–appropriate for all students, whether they are struggling or advanced. School districts that commit to implementation of RtI for students at both ends of the educational continuum need to embrace this concept when creating their educational plans and RtI strategies.

REFERENCES

Coil, Carolyn. (2008). *Coil RTI progress monitoring forms™ for gifted learners.* Marion, IL: Pieces of Learning.

Coil, Carolyn. (2009). *Differentiation, RTI, and achievement: How they work together.* Marion, IL: Pieces of Learning.

Gavin, M. K., & Adelson, J. L. (2008). Mathematics, elementary. In J. A. Plucker & C. M. Callahan (Eds.), *Critical issues and practices in gifted education: What the research says,* (pp. 367-394). Waco, TX: Prufrock Press.

Reis, S. M., Burns, D., & Renzulli, J. (1992). *Curriculum compacting: The complete guide to modifying the regular curriculum for high ability students.* Mansfield Center, CT: Creative Learning Press.

Rimm, S. B. (1997). Underachievement syndrome: A national epidemic. In N. Colangelo, & G. A. Davis, (Eds.), *Handbook of gifted education* (2nd ed., pp. 416-434). Boston, MA: Allyn and Bacon.

Slade, M. (2002, July). Presentation at the 2002 Summer Institute for Academic Diversity. Charlottesville, VA.

Tomlinson, C. A. (2003). *Fulfilling the promise of the differentiated classroom.* Alexandria, VA: Association for Supervision and Curriculum Development.

Winebrenner, S. (2001). *Teaching gifted kids in the regular classroom.* Minneapolis, MN: Free Spirit.

Chapter 2

What Is Intelligence?

Ideas about intelligence have changed over time and from culture to culture. At one time, the fire bringer and/or the fast runner were prized for their gifts. Theories from Terman to Gardner have ranged from ideas about intelligence from IQ-based to being far reaching in multiple domains.

As the theories of intelligence change, so do the definitions of giftedness. Dr. Francis Galton, influenced by Charles Darwin, first proposed a theory of general intelligence. For Galton, intelligence had a biological basis that could be studied by measuring reaction times to certain cognitive tasks. In France, Dr. Alfred Binet (Binet & Simon, 1916) believed that intelligence quotient (IQ) was not a real thing with specific identifiable properties, but rather an average of numerous dissimilar abilities. The idea of having numerous abilities that were dissimilar opened the door for the idea of multiple intelligences.

Dr. Lewis Terman, creator of the Stanford Binet Test of Intelligence, used IQ to define giftedness (Terman, 1916). His test has been used to support both the unilinear and multiple intelligence theories. His definition of gifted was an IQ of 140 or higher on the Stanford Binet or an equivalent measure on a similar test of intelligence.

In the United States in the early 1900s at the onset of testing, it was held that intelligence could be measured with a test. The range of scores could be displayed on the bell-shaped curve as a visible representation of the range of intelligence. The score on a test could determine what rank you held in the armed services, which college or profession you might enter, or in which classes you could enroll. Many schools used test scores to identify giftedness.

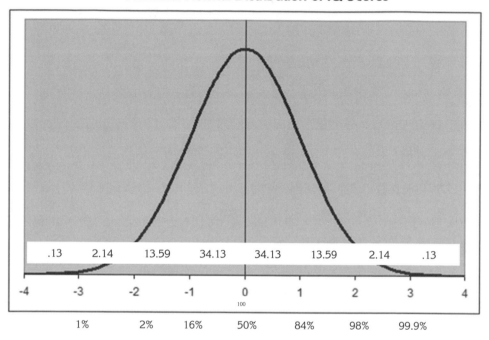

Figure 2.1. Standard Normal Distribution

In Figure 2.1, the bell curve illustrates the average range of intelligence (IQs) is from 85 to 115 with the mean of 100. Between 1-2 standard deviations above the mean, the range is 115-130. Within this range, are the high average to high above average students. There needs to be recognition that there is a range of giftedness beyond 130 IQ. The range, like that for the average, is from mildly gifted, moderately gifted, to profoundly gifted.

Our ideas about intelligence have been modified over time. Dr. J. P. Guilford believed that the mind was like a huge rubik's cube. Guilford believed that the mind had many different facets (Meeker, 1969). One facet included the way we learn, another was the level of thinking in which we are engaged, and the other is the complexity of thought. One could be more or less intelligent in a number of different ways with different combinations. This opened the door for multiple intelligences.

The facet including the way we learn demonstrated that the *semantic* learner excels through words. The semantic learner would probably choose to read about a topic in order to learn it.

The *symbolic* learner is facile with numbers, phonics, and symbols. This learner looks at the parts, looks at the patterns, figures, and "gets it."

Figural learners need to touch or manipulate in order to learn about the topic. They need to draw it, mold it, physically put the puzzle together, or carve it out.

Behavioral learners need to dig in and learn by experiencing. Behavioral learners actually must "do it." They learn by role playing or delving into the experience.

How one processes learning is a key to intelligence. Because one learner needs to read about the information and another must act it out does not mean that one is more or less intelligent than the other. They both may be intelligent, but process information quite differently. School learning has traditionally been semantic and symbolic learning, and thus it has been easier to classify as gifted those semantic and symbolic students who learn rapidly.

Categories of Intelligence

Dr. Howard Gardner (1993) took the idea of multiple intelligences and demonstrated that people may have a predominant intelligence—a way in which they learn best. His research was done with normal children and adults as well as those who were experts, gifted, those who had brain damage, and people from diverse cultures. He specified that there are a number of intelligences: linguistic, logical-mathematical, visual-spatial, musical-rhythmic, bodily-kinesthetic, interpersonal, intrapersonal, and naturalist. Gardner believes that psychometric tests address only linguistic and logical intelligence and some aspects of spatial intelligence. The paper and pencil format, or most tests, rules out many types of intelligences that are significant in real life.

Gardner's model is not to be used to construe that everyone is gifted. It does imply that all may have a preferred way of learning and that giftedness requires a preferred way to excel in one or more areas. Our job as educators is to find the way in which students best process information so that they may learn all that they are capable of learning. This may or may not involve testing. Some students may have gifts or talents in specific areas or even in multiple areas.

Dr. Robert Sternberg's (1984) triarchic theory of intelligence suggests that there are three components of intelligence: analytic, creative, and practical. Only one of these, analytic, is actually measured on most tests. He emphasizes the importance of balancing the analytic intelligence with the creative and the practical.

Dr. Art Costa (1988) defines intelligent behaviors. Those behaviors include:

- persistence;
- decreasing impulsivity;
- listening to others with understanding and empathy;
- cooperative thinking, social intelligence;
- flexibility in thinking;
- metacognition, awareness about one's own thinking;
- striving for accuracy and precision;
- sense of humor;
- questioning and problem posing;
- drawing on past knowledge and applying it to new situations;
- risk taking;
- using all the senses;
- ingenuity, originality, insightfulness, creativity;
- wonderment, inquisitiveness, curiosity, the enjoyment of problem solving; and
- a sense of efficacy as a thinker.

Categories of Giftedness

In 1972, the U.S. Office of Education commissioned Sidney Marland to do a study of gifted in the United States. Marland (1972) defined gifted as children who possessed:

- general intellectual ability,
- specific academic aptitude,
- creative and productive thinking,
- leadership ability,
- visual and performing arts, and/or
- psychomotor ability.

Thus, a person could be gifted in multiple ways.

What We Know About Intelligence and Giftedness

What we do know is that intelligence and giftedness are ill defined. *Real* intelligence is not able to be adequately measured and is influenced by both biological and environmental factors. Although there is much controversy surrounding the biological factors, evidence suggests that genetic variation has a significant impact on IQ. Adoption studies indicate that there is an IQ correlation between twins and full siblings that does not exist with adoptive siblings (Turkheimer, 1991). Family environmental factors may play a part in childhood IQ, but by late adolescence, the correlation disappears.

We know that intelligence and giftedness are elusive at best, but they must be recognized and nurtured for them to develop and to be utilized. Each person has a profile of strengths and weaknesses that are a result of learning and development. These differences are in intelligence, creativity, cognitive style, and motivation, as well as the capacity to process information, communicate, and relate to others. Giftedness includes an excess in one or more of these areas.

Dr. David Sousa (2009) has published the most recent brain research. It indicates that the processes in the development of the prefrontal cortex vary among children with different levels of intelligence and that those with superior intelligence show the greatest rates of change. (The prefrontal cortex is the area of abstract reasoning, planning, and decision-making.) Therefore, IQ relates in part to the maturation of the cortex, and people with high intelligence scores tend to have larger than average regions of the cortex. Research found that other brain regions in the parietal lobe are also involved in the development of intelligence. Sousa (2009) states, "Stimuli enter the rear of the brain, integrate in the center, and are interpreted by the frontal lobes. Gifted individuals may be able to do this faster and with greater accuracy than typical individuals" (p. 27).

What does this mean for gifted students? Dr. Sousa indicates that we need to look more closely at education in the primary and intermediate grades. Is the learning environment challenging? creative? He feels that what happens in classrooms might actually raise or lower a student's IQ.

Dr. Sousa cites the increasing percentage of gifted students who drop out of high school as a disturbing trend. Ways gifted students can benefit from appropriate curriculum, teaching strategies, and products that can challenge them include:

- differentiated curriculum beyond grade-level standards;
- differentiated instruction;
- using a faster pace, greater independence in study and thought, and increased complexity and depth in subject content;
- a supportive learning environment also addressing social and emotional needs; and
- curriculum content initiatives for gifted learners including acceleration when needed, curriculum compacting, and flexible grouping.

Instructional processes include:

- higher level thinking,
- creative thinking,
- problem-based learning,

- independent study,
- tiered assignments,
- discovery-based teaching that focuses on long term memory processing, and
- appropriate products for gifted learners.

As cognitive neuroscience continues to evolve, updating our knowledge of how the brain learns, it is important to integrate this information into schools and meet the learning needs of all students, including the gifted.

Gifted students are not all alike. They have a range of abilities and talents that exceed average expectations or curriculum designs. The gifted have an excess of ability permitting them to see things differently, learn at accelerated rates, and process information at a different pace.

In our search for equity and excellence, our efforts have predominately aimed for equity, ignoring excellence. Nationally, it has even been perceived that excellence is elitist in academics, yet highly valued in other areas such as athletics. In the Olympics, no nation proclaims that they will send a mixed-ability team. There are tryouts and competitions with eliminations. Every participating nation sends its best athletes–those who are at the top. In academics, it is quite a different matter. We often make fun of our brightest students and make being smart undesirable. Part of this is due to the fact that misconceptions abound about giftedness.

Myths and Misconceptions About Gifted Students

Gifted students will make it on their own.

The fact is that without help and special provisions gifted students more often adapt to regular classroom expectations. In some instances, it is not too bright to be too bright, especially when being rewarded for finishing early means more of the same work.

Gifted students enjoy teaching others.

This is true only when the other student is also gifted. Because gifted students process information at such a rapid pace and in such a different manner, they do not understand why the struggling student does not catch on. Their impatience grows, and the struggling student may feel even worse for her inability to see the answer.

Gifted students come from predominately white, middle, and upper-middle class families.

Gifted students come in all colors, from all ethnic and economic groups, and all geographic locations. Some may be discriminated against due to the identification procedures used. For example, if the test used to identify giftedness is primarily a language test, the child who is just learning the language may be at a disadvantage if a different language is spoken at home.

Gifted children cannot be identified before third grade.

Young gifted children can be observed and identified before third grade. Third grade tends to be a time when schools test students, and they have documentation to justify placing students in a gifted program. Young gifted children are like sponges, soaking up all the information that is in their paths. They tend to have large vocabularies, ask questions that don't have answers in the textbooks, and may be precocious in one or more areas.

Gifted students will excel.

Gifted students who get straight **A**'s may be the students who are learning the least. When compared with others in their class, gifted students may be learning nothing new. Even though they are at the head of their class, these students may already know most of the material. They may have learned it years before and have learned nothing new. There may be no challenge, no depth or complexity, no rigor for the gifted student without differentiating the curriculum. When looking at student potential compared to actual achievement, gifted students may be the biggest underachievers in the class. This promotes the idea that learning should come easily. Gifted students who have not learned how to grapple with new information, or who have not learned how to organize their time, or who cannot chunk assignments, may eventually give up, thinking that their giftedness has failed them or that they are imposters.

Gifted children need to do all of the regular work to solidify the information.

Relearning information is not what the gifted child wants or needs. Relearning produces sloppy work, careless errors, and a negative attitude towards schoolwork. Because gifted students learn in 1-5 repetitions, they need less skill and drill work and more application and research to find and apply new information.

Gifted students should not receive additional opportunities. If we allow the gifted students to participate in additional opportunities, then other students will want to do the same things.

If other students can do the assigned or chosen work that gifted students are required to do, then they should be doing that work or assignment. If the class could, would, should do the work or assignment given to the gifted, then why aren't they? Curriculum for the gifted needs to be differentiated so that it stretches the gifted student to struggle with difficult concepts, to promote thinking, and to challenge the student with different ways of presenting the newly learned information.

Gifted students do not need help.

Gifted students may be hesitant to raise their hands or to ask for help when they don't know something, because they presume that they should know it all. They need to know that there is nothing bad about not knowing the answer, and it is quite all right to ask for help when unsure of how to proceed. There will be times when it is unhealthy to not ask the question and instead worry about a situation or problem. Everyone needs assistance from time to time. It may be in an academic area or a social and emotional area. Gifted students may need assistance, but they may be leery about seeking help.

Identifying gifted students will make other children feel badly.

We don't worry about children who are selected to participate on sports teams. They try out, and the coaches choose those students who have the potential to excel in that area. Some students are not selected, but that is rarely questioned. Students try out for musical options. Not everyone can be first chair in the orchestra. Why then is there a negative connotation when we identify students who need a different curriculum? Dr. Stephanie Tolan, co-author of *Guiding the Gifted Child* stated, "You don't have the moral right to hold one child back to make another child feel better." When the gifted student is held back, he is the one who is learning to feel badly about his abilities because he is being punished by not being allowed to feel good about what he knows and can do. He is being asked in most cases to relearn what he already knows. He is being denied the chance to expand his knowledge and feel proud of what he can do. When there is no challenge or struggle to learn, we are sacrificing that student's learning potential.

Gifted children are easy to raise and are easy to teach.

Gifted students experience asynchronous development. Their chronological age, intellectual, physical, social, and emotional development may all be at different levels. The 7-year-old may be able to compute math problems at an advanced level yet write illegibly and cry often. They question things that other children do not comprehend. They worry about world problems and issues. Teaching and parenting gifted children takes skill and knowledge of their special abilities and needs.

Accelerating a gifted student is harmful.

Research in *A Nation Deceived* verifies that acceleration does not harm the child who is advanced. Acceleration is a powerful educational tool that is low in cost, can be flexible to match the pace of the learner, and requires participation of parents. It is more than just grade acceleration. According to Southern and Jones (2004) in *A Nation Deceived* there are 18 types of acceleration. Grade-skipping is not the only possibility.

Types of acceleration include:

- early admission to kindergarten;
- early admission to first grade;
- grade-skipping;
- continuous progress,
- self-paced instruction;
- subject-matter acceleration/partial acceleration;
- combined classes;
- curriculum compacting;
- telescoping curriculum;
- mentoring;
- extracurricular programs;
- correspondence courses;
- early graduation;
- concurrent/dual enrollment;
- advanced placement,
- credit by examination;
- acceleration in college; and
- early entrance into middle school, high school, or college.

(Southern & Jones, 2004).

Conclusion

Although our understanding of giftedness is difficult to define and filled with misconceptions and misunderstandings, we must recognize its importance and embrace the opportunity to make changes so that all children, including the gifted, have an appropriate education.

REFERENCES

Binet, A. & Simon, T. (1973). *The development of intelligence in children (the Binet-Simon Scale* (El Kite, Trans.). New York, NY: Arno Press. (Original work published 1916).

Costa, A. (1988). Teaching for intelligence: Recognizing and encouraging skillful thinking and behavior. *Transforming Education, 18,* 22.

Gardner, H. (1993). *Frames of mind: The theory of multiple intelligences.* New York, NY: Basic Books.

Marland, S. P., Jr. (1972). *Education of the gifted and talented: Report to the Congress of the United States by the U.S. Commissioner of Education and background papers submitted to the U.S. Office of Education,* 2 vols. Washington, DC: U.S. Government Printing Office. (Government Documents, Y4.L 11/2: G36).

Meeker, M. (1969). *The structure of intellect: Its uses and interpretation.* Columbus, OH: Charles Merrill.

Sousa, D. (2009). *How the gifted brain learns* (2nd ed.). Thousand Oaks, CA: Corwin Press.

Southern W. T., & Jones, E. D. (2004). Types of acceleration: Dimensions and issues. In N. Colangelo, S. G. Assouline, & M. U. M. Gross (Eds.), *A nation deceived: How schools hold back America's brightest* students (Vol. 2, pp. 5-12). Iowa City: The University of Iowa, The Connie Belin & Jacqueline N. Blank International Center for Gifted Education and Talent Development.

Sternberg, R. J. (1982). *Handbook of human intelligence.* Cambridge, UK: Cambridge University Press.

Sternberg, R. (1984). *Beyond I.Q.; A triarchic theory of human intelligence.* New York, NY: Cambridge University Press.

Terman, L. (1916). *The measurement of intelligence.* Boston, MA: Houghton Mifflin.

Turkheimer, E. (1991). Individual and group differences in adoption studies of IQ. *Psychological Bulletin, 110,* 392–405.

How to Identify Right Tier 2 & Right Tier 3 Gifted Students

For many years, gifted programs have targeted certain measures of intelligence to identify gifted students in their districts. And these measures often identify students who show potential in reading/language arts or math or demonstrate general intelligence. But no matter what measure is used, districts have found that many students of promise are not identified using these traditional measures. The easiest gifted students to identify are white, middle-class, suburban children because standard school achievement measures that find them are so often used. Some districts use an IQ measure, and that can be helpful at times. Increasingly, districts have only the state high-stakes test to use as an identifier, which, for many reasons, may not be beneficial in identifying Right Tier 2 and Tier 3 students.

Along with any district-administered tests, our suggestion is to train teachers to look beyond test results to behaviors in the classroom. Specific behaviors can be very effective identifiers for Response to Intelligence.

One of the best yet saddest examples from one gifted coordinator's experience in gifted education occurred many years ago. A fifth grade teacher told her during the identification process that he had a good candidate for the gifted program. The child was a culturally diverse boy who demonstrated many advanced learning characteristics in the classroom (the teacher had training in gifted education so he was alert to these characteristics). The teacher and the coordinator looked at his scores used on the district-determined identification measures and matrix and discovered he fell just short of qualifying.

The coordinator was new to the district and to the program so she consulted the curriculum director who said the scores were not there, and the child could not qualify. This upsetting situation awakened the coordinator to the limitations of scores and other typical measures used to identify children for gifted programs.

Gifted education specialists must continue to use whatever measures are agreed upon by a district, but they also must look beyond those measures to observable behaviors in the classroom, both positive and negative. Then Tier 2 and Tier 3 gifted students can be more accurately identified.

Characteristics of Gifted Children

Following are examples of general characteristics of gifted children and how they may be used to identify at-risk gifted children:

- **Learns Rapidly**

A typical characteristic of a gifted child is the ability to learn quickly. Many complete assignments early and demonstrate *by their behavior* that they are ready for alternate material. Unfortunately, some teachers, seeing that some students finish quickly, proceed to give students *more* work. It is *different* work that they need, not more work. Other students may understand concepts quickly and proceed to disrupt others when they are finished. That may be an indication of the need for gifted curriculum and instruction. Still others may have processing problems that interfere with book learning but demonstrate that they learn rapidly in their own ways and in their own areas of high potential. This is a clear indication of the need for RtI for gifted learners.

- **High Level Verbal Skills**

Students who display the ability to express themselves clearly using advanced vocabulary are often identified as having gifted potential. However, some students learn how to use vocabulary to intimidate those in authority or to manipulate others for their own purposes. They can become very clever in their use of language. That, too, is an indication of high potential. Another indicator identifies students with vocabulary skills particular to a given culture but not the mainstream (Standard English) vocabulary. Finally, we have those students who are easily able to switch between two (or more) languages using elements of both and following correct grammatical rules. This is called *code-switching* and can be an indicator of accelerated language development when used in an advanced way.

- **Reasoning Ability**

Students who show high potential may be able to use advanced reasoning at an early age. They may have rapid insight into cause and effect relationships and may enjoy displaying that ability by seeing relationships others do not and may even disrupt the classroom with answers and interruptions.

- **Intensity and Sensitivity**

A clear indicator of high potential is the student who displays a high degree of intensity and sensitivity in the classroom. In *Living With Intensity* various contributors well known in the gifted education field discuss the varied forms of intensity which are indicative of the gifted individual (Daniels & Piechowski, 2008). Significant are the five types of overexcitabilities as defined by Dr. Kazimierz Dabrowski (1970) that can be commonly exhibited in the classroom by students. Any combination of two or more of the following can indicate giftedness and are indicators of the need for Right Tiers 2 and 3 Gifted Intervention:

Psychomotor Overexcitability–Kids who *have* to move–they learn best when they are moving; they have a surplus of energy, love physical activity; they can be compulsive talkers and chatterers. Sometimes these students are misdiagnosed as ADHD.

Sensual Overexcitability–These children are intensely aware of the world around them; they have heightened sensory awareness. They may love or hate certain textures, smells, sounds etc. Music and/or art can move them to tears. They appreciate beautiful objects, words, music, etc.

Intellectual Overexcitability–This overexcitability is most directly associated with giftedness. Students who display this characteristic have a passion for learning. They like probing questions, logical thinking, and have a capacity for sustained intellectual pursuit. They may be voracious readers and independent thinkers and seek understanding and truth.

Imaginational Overexcitability–These students are the dreamers and the seekers with heightened imaginations, living in the world of creativity. They may like fantasy and magic stories, may be very dramatic, and may have a heightened sense of humor–sometimes bizarre!

Emotional Overexcitability–These students demonstrate intense positive or negative feelings–perhaps living on a roller coaster of emotion. They are very sensitive to others' feelings and have an intense commitment to their perception of right and wrong. They may have a deep commitment to social issues at an early age.

Whenever students display several of these overexcitabilities it is a clear indication of the possibility for Right Tiers 2 and 3 interventions. Many times students who display these intensities have *not* been identified for a district gifted program so the classroom teacher becomes a critical identifier for these children.

- **Wide and Diverse Interests, Passion for Learning, and Other Skills**

Another possible identifier includes children with wide and diverse interests. They may want to know *everything* about a topic of interest. These interests may not be part of mainstream education, yet need to be recognized. These students have a passion about their area and not, perhaps, about the academic topic under discussion. Whenever a teacher finds a student with a passion about something, it is time to pay attention. This child might be gifted.

Other areas that need to be considered for gifted identification include high level figural skills, excellent memory (sometimes they remember things you wish they would forget!), high levels of concentration on topics of interest (student interest, not teacher interest or district curriculum), systems thinker (perhaps inventing their own systems) and independence in work and study (including non-conformity).

Finally, creativity skills including high levels of curiosity and keen observation and the ability to see things in new and different ways are good clues that there is high potential, no matter what else the child brings to the academic table. Creative students may display an advanced sense of humor that can even appear to be somewhat bizarre. The creative students are the ones who get the jokes and love puns and wordplays.

The Bottom Line

There are standardized tests that attempt to identify gifted children. Some of them are more effective than others. However, they have significant limitations. Various estimates conclude that a significant percentage of gifted students are missed on standardized testing (and that tests only look at a student during one day's time (Coleman, 2003). If these scores or scores on individual intelligence tests are available, educators must look for a *scatter score* with extreme highs and lows that may help identify at-risk gifted students.

Also, educators must check for academic prior knowledge when students are from another culture or speak a different language. When teachers understand the cultural background of a student, they may also be more effective in identifying behaviors as well as challenging them in classrooms. For example, students with limited academic background knowledge may need scaffolding from initiatives such as *Building Academic Vocabulary* in order to bring them up to speed (Marzano & Pickering, 2005).

Scaffolding refers to a structure of supports such as tutors or introductory tools to build on what the student knows so that he/she may experience success and growth. Too often students with limited background can be placed in gifted programs and then "fail" or drop out of the program. It may be because they lacked the tools to be successful and are at a different place than children from enriched environments.

Dr. George Betts and Dr. Maureen Neihart created profiles of gifted and talented based on their behaviors. They have recently revised their profiles (Betts & Neihart, 2009). They divided students into six typologies, discussed their feelings and attitudes, their behaviors, and their needs. These profiles are effective in locating gifted and talented students regardless of their backgrounds. The six typologies based on their behaviors include:

- the Successful student,
- the Challenging student,
- the Underground student,
- the At-Risk student,
- the Twice/Multi Exceptional student, and
- the Autonomous Learner.

Each typology includes the feelings and attitudes of the group, their typical behaviors, their social/emotional needs, how adults and peers perceive them, and what parents and schools can do to support them. Many who work with the gifted and talented find this research invaluable in their support of these students.

However, whether a student is urban or rural, ADHD or Aspergers, bilingual or homeless, participating in gifted program services or not (etc.), the best way for teachers to identify them is to try to catch them thinking! It is the quickest way to identify a child with high potential. Make sure curriculum and instruction focus on the *students* rather than the *content*. The content should meet the needs of the students, rather than the reverse!

Dr. Bertie Kingore (2001) created an effective instrument for identifying gifted children, K–8, in the regular classroom. In her Kingore Observation Inventory (KOI) 2nd Edition, she provides assessments, forms, procedures, and interpretations along with differentiation aids to support classroom teachers in finding and serving gifted children.

Conclusion

Remember, all students need the opportunity to learn and *grow* in schools, and every child, including the gifted, has the *right* to grow at least one year for every year spent in school. Every child must be given curriculum and instruction *at his or her level* so that all students develop the skills to survive in their world. If we in education truly want to provide an intelligent response to meet the learning needs of *all* students we must provide a continuum of services and appropriate curriculum and instruction for all students in the classroom. In this way, we are creating a response to intervention no matter who the child is.

Effective differentiation provides for Tiers 1, 2, AND 3 on *both* sides of the continuum, not just for struggling students, but for every child. Then, and only then, RtI, a promising reform movement in education, will be successful with *all* students in the classroom. And finally, students with gifted potential will also have their needs met through their education.

Gifted students will not be left behind.

REFERENCES

Betts, G. T., & Neihart, M. (2009, November). *The revised profiles of the gifted and talented: A research-based approach.* Paper presented at the annual meeting of the National Association for Gifted Children, St. Louis, MO.

Coleman, M. R. (2003). *The identification of students who are gifted* (ERIC Digest #644.). Arlington, VA: The ERIC Clearinghouse on Disabilities and Gifted Education.

Dabrowski, K. (with Kawczak, A., & Piechowski, M.). (1970). *Mental growth through positive disintegration.* London, England: Gryf.

Daniels, S., & Piechowski, M. (Eds.). (2008). *Living with intensity.* Scottsdale, AZ: Great Potential Press.

Kingore, B. (2001). *Kingore observation inventory* (2nd ed.). Austin, TX: Professional Associates Publishing.

Marzano, R. J., & Pickering, D. J. (2005). *Building academic vocabulary: Teacher's manual.* Alexandria VA: ASCD.

Chapter 4

Survival in the Classroom: Academic and Affective/ Behavioral

The overarching purpose of the NEW RtI (Response to Intelligence Model™) is to improve educational outcomes for all students (general education, special education, compensatory, and gifted). The NEW RtI requires high-quality curriculum, continuous review of student progress, and collaboration between general education teachers, specialists, and parents. The NEW RtI is an opportunity for students with special needs, including gifted students, to be recognized so that their education can be appropriately addressed with high-quality, standards-based instruction and interventions that are matched to their needs.

Gifted students have special needs; they are *at* risk of learning the least in the classroom. Teachers, administrators, and parents frequently feel that since the gifted child is getting the highest grades in the class and not causing any trouble they are doing "fine." It is often believed that these students will make it on their own; they do not need special help. How wrong this is!

RtI supports a continuum of evidence-based tiered interventions with increasing levels of complexity, depth, and pacing for academic achievement. The tiered approach is not new to gifted education. Tomlinson (1999) promoted tiered lessons and units. The tiered approach addresses the increasing diversity that we see in our student populations.

A continuum can be applied not only to academic needs, but also to social and emotional needs, or behavioral needs as specified by the traditional Response to Intervention model. By looking at the model in Figure 4.1, we can begin to plan for what needs to happen in the classroom.

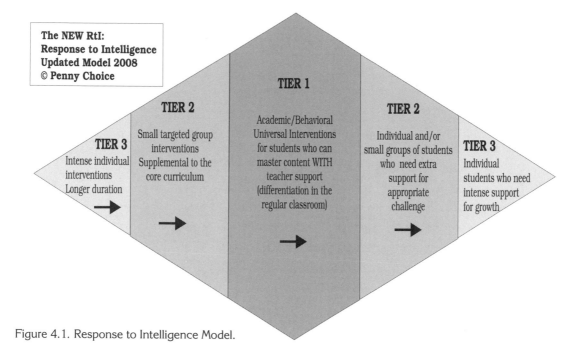

Figure 4.1. Response to Intelligence Model.

Objective for struggling students*: To be successful at Tier 1 or higher.*

Objective for advanced students*: To receive appropriate challenge for growth (and skill development) at least 1 year for every year spent in school.*

Academic Differentiation

The concept of differentiation is not new. Differentiation began in gifted education long before it became a general education buzzword. At its heart lies the idea that students are individuals with different learning styles, different levels of readiness to learn, and different areas of interest. Opportunities to learn must be differentiated in order to engage each student in tasks that are meaningful and offer appropriate challenge. Gifted students may not be gifted in everything, just as children with learning differences may not have difficulty with every area of learning. Flexibility is an important aspect of differentiation. Instruction must be adjusted based on student needs rather than having students adjust to standard curriculum.

Early intervention needs to occur in order to not only address the young child's learning needs, but also to build on the strengths of the child. It is critical to intervene to prevent problems, to lessen existing problems, and to guarantee that the child's strengths do not disappear or diminish. Too often early intervention only addresses the problem area(s) without looking at the area(s) of strength. For gifted children it is imperative to recognize and support strengths. This can be done through the New RtI approach. By nurturing the child's strengths, we are providing the key to continuing success especially when identification for gifted programming does not occur until later grades. This is needed for ALL gifted children, but especially vital for the continued success of children from underserved populations (children who are culturally or linguistically diverse or are economically disadvantaged; Coleman & Hughes, 2009).

In the Response to Intelligence Model™ Tier 1 represents what most students should know and be able to do as a result of the content for their age and grade level in the general education classroom. What is the core or essential information for this unit or lesson? What do I (the teacher) want students to know, understand, and be able to do as a result of learning this content? Tomlinson states that curriculum must (Batsche, et al., 2005):

- focus on rich, profound ideas of the discipline;
- engage the students emotionally and cognitively;
- require students to solve problems;

- address issues;
- create products; and
- be relevant to their lives.

What is the big picture? What is worth knowing and doing? How will students become engaged in the learning and relate the learning to their lives? Tier 1 provides the basics of curriculum that is high quality, scientifically based, and differentiated to meet students' needs. It is assumed that 80-90% of the students will achieve high levels of growth at this stage (Medina, 2009). Yet, to assume that all students will need the same curriculum, instructional methods, or time to learn is not only poorly conceived, but also very ineffective.

It is essential that general education classrooms have high-quality learning opportunities, use dynamic assessments, and implement monitoring that documents students' progress and mastery of the curriculum. Thus, the general education classroom must embrace and support differentiation. It is essential at Tier 1. In fact, the more differentiation is utilized in Tier 1, fewer students will need the special provisions at Tier 2.

Again, flexibility is key. Assessment with grouping and re-grouping is constantly occurring based on student interests, prior experiences with the content, and learning styles. Students will learn at different rates in different content areas. This is normal and to be expected. Because of this, anchor activities and extension enrichment activities or, "What should I do when I finish?" activities must be available. These activities can sometimes be found as extensions to the lesson in the text. These activities also may be related to content and extend thinking, problem solving, or result in products that expand on the student's knowledge. They should be exciting, engaging, and challenging learning experiences, not just busy work.

Opportunities to differentiate may include, but are not limited to:

- thinking at different levels;
- open-ended opportunities for responses;

- tiered opportunities to respond (based on prior knowledge (i.e., graphic organizers with varying degrees of difficulty);
- product choices;
- primary sources;
- research studies;
- problem solving; and
- cluster grouping of gifted students.

Tier 2 is for students who need additional support and opportunities based on their needs and rate of learning. This Tier is for more advanced differentiation at both ends of the learning continuum. Tier 2 students on both the left and right need more intensive instruction with matching supplemental work. Differentiation at this level is required to allow for modifications in time and content. On the Left, it may apply to students not making adequate progress in the core curriculum. On the Right it may apply to students for whom the core curriculum is redundant. They are in need of increasingly intensive instruction matched to their needs on the basis of levels of performance and rates of progress.

Right Tier 2 has a need for a different kind of instruction and decreasing emphasis on the general curriculum. These students learn at a faster pace, need less repetitions, grasp the idea more quickly, have mastered much of the core curriculum in Tier 1, and are ready to move on to more advanced concepts. Core curriculum learning for these students comes more easily. Small homogeneous groups or individual instruction are appropriate in this Tier. Right Tier 2 requires supplemental work that is challenging and continues the instruction through depth and complexity of content with rigorous thinking. Using compacting, extensions to the curriculum can be planned. Compacting consists of identifying the learning objectives that need to be mastered. Assessments are offered to those who think they already know the material. Based on the successful assessment results, mastered curricula is eliminated, and students move into Right Tier 2 and are offered curriculum extensions in order to avoid repetition or review of mastered material.

The format of this group may be a replacement class, self-contained gifted class, a separate school within a school, or a separate school. It includes cluster grouping, cooperative learning grouping, and cross-ability or –age grouping. For small districts, it may mean grouping students together from multiple grade levels for replacement classes. Replacement classes are classes that typically are held in a content area that is occurring at the same time in the regular classroom. Instead of completing the standard math curriculum, the replacement class focus may be on accelerated math content and skills. The replacement class meets daily, and the teacher of that class issues the homework and the grade for the content area.

Right Tier 2 students can complete anchor activities and extensions to the curriculum during the time that others require to learn the basic curriculum. Thus, some acceleration works well for these students. Advanced resources are options for this group. Exposure to inquiry experiences, problem-based learning, debate, future studies, contracting work through compacting, or competitions work well in this Tier. Concept-based curriculum is desirable.

Because the knowledge is advanced for these students, it does not mean that they do not need teacher time. These students still require teacher guidance and instruction to learn the steps of research, to learn pacing of self and of curriculum, to learn organizational strategies, and to delve deeper and more complexly into the concept or topic.

They also need time to explore the affective implications of their gifts. Becoming familiar with the overexcitibilities and their implications is useful to these students. This group can benefit from relaxation techniques and brain research and its implications. Because of the needed guidance, the instructor for this group of students should be one who has had course work in gifted education and gifted curriculum.

Gifted students may not be gifted in everything, just as children with learning differences may not have difficulty with every area of learning. Therefore, a gifted student may also be placed in Left Tier 2 for additional support and guidance focusing on instruction and supplemental work that is needed to grasp, reintroduce, or reinforce a concept or skill. Therefore, communication between the general education teacher and the gifted education specialist is essential.

The students in **Tier 3** require intensive, more individualized intervention. This group should be comprised of very few students.

The students at the Left end of the continuum are not making adequate progress in the core curriculum and must be provided with increasingly intensive instruction matched to *their* needs on the basis of levels of performance and rates of progress.

Students in Left Tier 3 are those who struggle and need explicit, step-by-step assistance to learn the material. The core must be replaced with individually tailored, appropriate, engaging learning.

Right Tier 3 students also need the core curriculum replaced. Right Tier 3 is delivered to individuals or very small groups of students who have intense needs that extend far beyond the curriculum of that grade level. Their advanced mastery of content dictates that they have increased time to devote to intensive study of an area. Because they already know the content, accelerated, concept-based content is needed. Its replacement could lead to independent study, research, problem solving, delving deeper into the content, exploration into related areas, acceleration options such as grade advancement, dual enrollment, early Advanced Placement classes or early college classes. Enrichment for these students is not appropriate.

Like Left Tier 3 students at the other end of the learning spectrum, these students deserve to have individual attention in order to have the opportunity to learn new content and to grapple with new, challenging information.

Right Tier 3 students need to be aware of their overexcitibilities and intensities, as well as how they affect their lives and those around them. They may need counseling help to deal with issues that affect their lives (perfectionism, underachievement, making friends, depression, etc.) Their teacher must have special training and/or classes in gifted education in order to provide the accelerated curriculum and guidance that is required at this level.

Moving to the Right

Teachers must work to move all students to the right. The goal for Left Tier 3 and Left Tier 2 is to move the student toward the proficiency level of Tier 1. Left Tier 3 has specific individual or group needs that dictate an intensive intervention. The replacement or substitution of core information may be considered. Left Tier 2 students need special help and extra support to be able to move to Tier 1.

The goal of Right Tier 2 and Right Tier 3 is to move the student beyond grade-level proficiency into new learning and challenging content.

Both Left and Right Tiers 2 and 3 have needs that call for increasing or decreasing of support as dictated by their readiness and pace of learning.

Tier 3 students at both ends of the learning continuum are few and have profound needs.

The purpose of the Response to Intelligence Model™ is not to move all students into Tier 1. The prime objective of this model is to move ALL students as far right as possible as dictated by the student's needs. With appropriate challenge, Right Tier 2 students may excel and require movement to Right Tier 3. Twice-exceptional students may need interventions at each level of the tiers.

How Do Students Qualify to Move to Differing Tiers?

Assessment and continuous monitoring of all students is a crucial component of the RtI puzzle. The purpose of assessment is to identify the strengths and needs of students. A balance of both formative and summative measures is needed to provide a complete and accurate picture of students' strengths and needs. The assessments provide the basis for our educational decisions about instruction and the necessary adjustments we need to consider. Teachers must pre-assess content knowledge and processes and assess effectiveness of on-going strategies through formative and summative assessments.

Assessment also provides the information that we need to monitor and document the effectiveness of our instruction once that has occurred. The assessments can be teacher, school, district, state, or nationally created and produced. They can be done informally through discussions and observations or formally by administered tests. Based on the results of pre-assessments teachers begin to plan strategies for content, process, and products related to the concept, unit, or topic.

Assessments may include, but are not limited to:

- observations
- book review
- booklet
- charts
- class or small group discussions
- checklists
- concept map/webs
- diagrams with labels
- experiments
- graphic organizers
- sample problems to solve
- oral summaries
- pre-tests
- vocabulary lists–students provide definition or match to definition
- problem solving
- portfolios
- questionnaires
- student-produced exhibits
- thumbs up, thumbs down
- Venn diagrams
- KWL charts
- ticket out the door (what I learned today, what questions I have)
- quizzes
- standardized tests

Following are progress monitoring forms for curriculum compacting and tiered lessons for gifted students. Included in the format are areas for pre-assessments, performance assessments, formative assessments, summative assessments, and suggestions for data-driven interventions–the Coil Progress Monitoring Forms™ for Gifted Learners (Coil, 2009).

Coil RTI Progress Monitoring Form™
Curriculum Compacting

Student's Name ____Caroline____

Targeted Skill, Knowledge, or Behavior
- Academic skills/knowledge that are easily assessed
  (Targeted skill/knowledge: Multiplication facts through 9 x 9

- Student claims to be "bored" and says she already knows the work

Pre-assessment: *(Record all that apply)*

Date(s) of Pre-assessment _____

Test score(s) 100% on pretest   Checklist Indicator(s) _____

Observation(s) _____

> Pretest covered all multiplication facts up to 9 x 9.

Performance Assessment

Below Expectation...Exceeds Expectations

Student has an understanding of some of the skills/ knowledge and could compact out of some of the work.	Student has an understanding of almost all of the skills/ knowledge and could usually compact out and do alternate activities.	Student has an understanding of all the skills/knowledge for this unit and could compact out of the entire unit and do alternate activities.	Student has mastered all the skills/ knowledge for this unit but has problems working independently doing higher level alternate activities.	Student has mastered all the skills/ knowledge for this unit and works well independently doing higher level alternate learning activities.

Strategies or Interventions: *(Describe or list below)*

Use the Curriculum Compacting strategy with this student. She will have a choice between two alternate activities or can come up with her own activity with teacher approval. Alternate activity choices:

1. Write a story entitled "The Land with No Multiplication." Be creative but include what you know about multiplication and its uses. Explain what might happen if people didn't know how to multiply.

2. Create a card game that requires both skill in multiplication and logical thinking. Make the game and write the rules. Then play it with a classmate.

from Differentiation, RTI, and Achievement How They Work Together Carolyn Coil, Marion IL: Pieces of Learning, 2009.

Formative Assessments *(Monitoring the Student's Response to Curriculum Compacting)*

Date __Monday___

Test score _____ Checklist Indicator(s) _____

Observation(s)

Caroline chooses to write a story called "The Land with No Multiplication."

Performance Assessment

Below Expectation...Exceeds Expectations

Student has an understanding of some of the skills/ knowledge and could compact out of some of the work.	Student has an understanding of almost all of the skills/ knowledge and could usually compact out and do alternate activities.	Student has an understanding of all the skills/knowledge for this unit and could compact out of the entire unit and do alternate activities.	Student has mastered all the skills/ knowledge for this unit but has problems working independently doing higher level alternate activities.	Student has mastered all the skills/ knowledge for this unit and works well independently doing higher level alternate learning activities.

Date __Tuesday-Friday___

Test score _____ Checklist Indicator(s) *Checkpoint with teacher each day*

Observation(s)

Caroline has difficulty working independently. Needs lots of guidance in writing the story.

Performance Assessment

Below Expectation...Exceeds Expectations

Student has an understanding of some of the skills/ knowledge and could compact out of some of the work.	Student has an understanding of some of the skills/ knowledge and could compact out of some of the work.	Student has an understanding of all the skills/knowledge for this unit and could compact out of the entire unit and do alternate activities.	Student has mastered all the skills/ knowledge for this unit but has problems working independently doing higher level alternate activities.	Student has mastered all the skills/ knowledge for this unit and works well independently doing higher level alternate learning activities.

Date __Monday of 2nd week___

Test score *100% on post test*   Checklist Indicator(s) _____

Observation(s)

Caroline remains above mastery level in multiplication facts. Completed the story. Needs to develop skills in independent learning.

Performance Assessment

Below Expectation...Exceeds Expectations

Student has an understanding of some of the skills/ knowledge and could compact out of some of the work.	Student has an understanding of almost all of the skills/ knowledge and could usually compact out and do alternate activities.	Student has an understanding of all the skills/knowledge for this unit and could compact out of the entire unit and do alternate activities.	Student has mastered all the skills/ knowledge for this unit but has problems working independently doing higher level alternate activities.	Student has mastered all the skills/ knowledge for this unit and works well independently doing higher level alternate learning activities.

from Differentiation, RTI, and Achievement How They Work Together Carolyn Coil, Marion IL: Pieces of Learning, 2009.

Summarize the Student's Response to Curriculum Compacting

1. Caroline exceeded grade level mastery in multiplication skills.

2. Story challenged her to develop higher-level thinking skills (application, analysis, synthesis, and evaluation).

3. Needs to work on independent learning skills.

4. She worked on the curriculum compacting alternate activity for one week.

Decision:

X Continue curriculum compacting as needed and appropriate

☐ Modify the intervention:

X Select / implement a new intervention
   Work on developing skills in independent learning.

☐ Move to the next tier (Tier _____)

☐ Refer for other special services:

from Differentiation, RTI, and Achievement How They Work Together Carolyn Coil, Marion IL: Pieces of Learning, 2009.

Coil RTI Progress Monitoring Form™
Tiered Lessons – Level 3

Student's Name _____ **Logan** _____

Targeted Skill, Knowledge, or Behavior
- <u>Any academic skill or standard that must be mastered:</u> Compound Words

Pre-assessment: *(Record all that apply)*

Date(s) of Pre-assessment _____

Test score(s) <u>90%</u> Checklist Indicator(s) _____
Identification of compound words
Observation(s)

> Student understands structure of compound words and knows how to use them. He is an excellent reader and writer.

Performance Assessment
Below Expectation..Exceeds Expectations

Student understands most of the topic or skill as indicated by pretest, checklist or observation.	Student understands almost all of the topic or skill as indicated by pretest, checklist or observation.	Student has mastered the topic or skill as indicated by pretest, checklist or observation. Needs to be challenged beyond this skill.	Student extends his/her knowledge or skill by working in Level 3 of the Tiered Lesson Plan format.	Student demonstrates higher level thinking, makes connections with other areas of learning, and uses advanced resources in his/her work.

Strategies or Interventions: *(Describe or list below)*

Use the Compound Words Tiered Lesson Plan – Level 3
— Whole group activities : Puzzle Pieces
— Dictionary of compound words
— Short story using imaginary compound words
— Walking words activity

from Differentiation, RTI, and Achievement How They Work Together Carolyn Coil, Marion IL: Pieces of Learning, 2009.

Formative Assessments *(Monitoring the Student's Response to Tiered Lessons)*

Date _____

Test score _____ Checklist Indicator(s) _____

Observation(s)
   Student participated in and enjoyed the whole group Puzzle Piece activity

Performance Assessment
Below Expectation...Exceeds Expectations

| Student understands most of the topic or skill as indicated by pretest, checklist or observation. | Student understands almost all of the topic or skill as indicated by pretest, checklist or observation. | Student has mastered the topic or skill as indicated by pretest, checklist or observation. Needs to be challenged beyond this skill. | Student extends his/her knowledge or skill by working in Level 3 of the Tiered Lesson Plan format. | Student demonstrates higher level thinking, makes connections with other areas of learning, and uses advanced resources in his/her work. |

Date _____

Test score _____ Checklist Indicator(s) _____

Observation(s)
   Was challenged when developing the dictionary.
   Difficulty in creative thinking.

Performance Assessment
Below Expectation...Exceeds Expectations

| Student understands most of the topic or skill as indicated by pretest, checklist or observation. | Student understands almost all of the topic or skill as indicated by pretest, checklist or observation. | Student has mastered the topic or skill as indicated by pretest, checklist or observation. Needs to be challenged beyond this skill. | Student extends his/her knowledge or skill by working in Level 3 of the Tiered Lesson Plan format. | Student demonstrates higher level thinking, makes connections with other areas of learning, and uses advanced resources in his/her work. |

Date _____

Test score _100%_____ Checklist Indicator(s) _____
   Identification of compound words
Observation(s)
   Challenged throughout tiered unit.
   Higher-level thinking demonstrated in short story.

Performance Assessment
Below Expectation...Exceeds Expectations

| Student understands most of the topic or skill as indicated by pretest, checklist or observation. | Student understands almost all of the topic or skill as indicated by pretest, checklist or observation. | Student has mastered the topic or skill as indicated by pretest, checklist or observation. Needs to be challenged beyond this skill. | Student extends his/her knowledge or skill by working in Level 3 of the Tiered Lesson Plan format. | Student demonstrates higher level thinking, makes connections with other areas of learning, and uses advanced resources in his/her work. |

from Differentiation, RTI, and Achievement How They Work Together Carolyn Coil, Marion IL: Pieces of Learning, 2009.

© **Pieces of Learning**

Summarize the Student's Response to Tiered Lessons and Units

1. Demonstrated mastery of structure of compound words. (90% - 100%)

2. Level 3 activities challenged this student.

3. Extended learning in creativity, word usage, and storytelling.

Decision:

X Successfully mastered the targeted skill, knowledge or behavior.

X Continue tiered lessons as needed and appropriate

    Continue to challenge this student with Level 3 tiered activities.

☐ Modify the intervention:

☐ Select / implement a new intervention

☐ Move to the next tier (Tier _____)

☐ Refer for other special services:

from Differentiation, RTI, and Achievement How They Work Together Carolyn Coil, Marion IL: Pieces of Learning, 2009.

Tiered Lesson Plan: Compound Words

Objectives or Standards

1. Students will recognize the structure of compound words.
2. Students will understand how and when compound words are used.
3. Students will create and use compound words.

Whole Class Activities

1. Demonstrate how compound words are created by using puzzle pieces with simple words to make compound words.

2. Listen to and sing the "Grammar Rock" song on compound words.

Assessment

❏All look and listen to teacher's demonstration.

❏All students singing and participating.

Level 1 Activities

1. Have these students make their own compound words from the puzzle pieces and write them on a sheet of paper.

2. Write 10 sentences using these compound words.

Assessment

❏All words created are compound words.

❏Correct spelling of words.
❏All words used.
❏Has 10 sentences.

Level 2 Activities

1. Generate a list of 10 new compound words. Highlight each part of the compound word with a different color.

2. Write two paragraphs using all 10 words.

Assessment

❏Has 10 compound words.
❏Parts are indicated correctly.

❏Paragraphs are in correct form with main idea.
❏All 10 words used.

from Activities & Assessments for the Differentiated Classroom. Carolyn Coil.
Pieces of Learning. www.piecesoflearning.com

© **Pieces of Learning**

Level 3 Activities

Assessment

1. Make a dictionary with 10 original compound words. Define and illustrate each.

☞ ❑Has 10 original words and definitions.
❑Words are illustrated.
❑In alphabetical order.

2. Write a short story using these 10 words.

☞ ❑Story uses all 10 words.
❑Has a plot with a beginning, middle and end.

Whole Class Culminating Activities

Assessment

1. Share products from Levels 1, 2 and 3.

❑Group participation

2. "Walking Words" activity where each student holds a word and finds a partner to make a compound word.

from *Activities & Assessments for the Differentiated Classroom. Carolyn Coil.*
Pieces of Learning. www.piecesoflearning.com

Based on the results of the assessment the teacher can begin to form groups for each of the five tiers. Questions to be considered:

- What form or configuration does the class take?
- Are there students who struggle with or who do not have a clue about the content?
- Are there students who need more supporting information in order to learn the content?
- Is the majority of the class ready to learn the age-appropriate information?
- Are there a few who already have content knowledge or who have mastered much of the content and are resident experts? Resident experts are students who know the subject well–know as much, if not more than the text. They *love* the topic and could bore most classmates to tears with their knowledge of the topic. As a teacher who is about to launch a study of the topic, consult the resident expert first. He/she has the latest data and the most resources.
- Are there students who need help with organizational skills?
- Is time management a problem for some students?
- Is there an opportunity for all students to learn something new and to develop persistence with enthusiasm for learning?

Progress of Tier 2 students is monitored more frequently than Tier 1. This is primarily so that ineffective interventions can be corrected in a timely manner. Are students responding to the intervention? Is progress being made? What adjustments to instruction/intervention are needed? Interventions are based on needs, and when those needs fluctuate or no longer exist, changes must be made.

Flexibility in grouping is a must. Once a child is comfortable with the information provided in Left Tier 2, is the child then able to transition into Tier 1? Or does the child in Right Tier 2 need extended opportunities to learn or, if appropriate, need to move to Right Tier 3? There may not be Right Tier 3 groups in all areas or even in all districts. In some instances, it may be only one child whose needs are beyond the group at either end. This is intensive intervention that supports students with extensive needs. Right Tier 3 may include radical acceleration options and/or community-based partnerships such as virtual learning courses.

Flexible Grouping

Flexible grouping is an essential component of managing the RtI classroom. The process of flexible grouping is not the same as tracking. With flexible grouping, students make constant changes. Sometimes students are grouped based on their learning styles. At other times they may be grouped based on their interests. Other times students are grouped based on their academic experiences and readiness to learn the content. Still other times the students may be gathered in groups based on their ability to work independently, to manage their time well, or to address their motivation issues. Affective concerns may be the source of regrouping students. At some point, they may have choice groups where they choose with whom they will work.

Grouping and expectations are fair only when we address the needs and differences that exist among students in our classrooms. The classroom community, as well as the home, acknowledges that differences do exist, and we try to address those differences to the best of our ability. The child with a hearing impairment may need a hearing device to facilitate his learning. The hearing device is not appropriate for everyone to have. Similarly, having extensions, rather than completing work that is repetitive and redundant, best serves the child who has already mastered the content. With gifted children, the development is very asynchronistic (uneven development that is out of sync with age peers) and needs continuous services.

In classrooms that have diverse learner needs, the Response to Intelligence Model™ is needed more than ever to address such diversity.

The teacher needs to set the stage explaining the expectation that not all will be doing the same thing at the same time. One can use the example of having several children together. Some of the infants develop their digestive systems earlier than others. To keep all of the infants on the same food, just because some systems are not yet advanced enough for solid foods, would leave those children with more developed systems hungry and waking more frequently, wanting more food. Other infants may have food allergies or different tastes. They need special diets or different choices available in order to meet their growing needs. Some require special formulas because of allergies; others can adapt to more varieties of baby food, while a few may need or prefer solid, adult food. The age and appropriateness of the diet is designed to meet the growing needs of the child so that nutritionally she has the best possible advantages of growing into a healthy adult. Not all children need the same food at the same time. We understand and support differing nutritional needs.

The same applies to intellectual and affective needs. In classrooms, some students need to be on special diets to promote their growth, much like infants. Students are able to chew and digest the content at different rates and at different times.

Personal tastes also vary and should be considered. While some students enjoy acting out a story, others may prefer to illustrate the story, write a different ending, put the story in a cartoon format, or create a rap.

Behavioral Management

Classroom management is one of the most common reasons that teachers feel uncomfortable with grouping and regrouping. To manage the class, the stage needs to be set with clear expectations. Let students know your expectations up front. For younger students, model what you expect to see, hear, and have done. Have students practice moving from group to group. You are the teacher. You know when gasoline and fire are together they do not mix. You can control grouping so that these two are not in the same group. You are in charge and can do that. Have supplies neatly organized and in place so they are accessible. Have affective rubrics like the one on the next page that grade the process and progress, not just the finished product.

Task Rubric

Work Habits	1	2	3	4
Stays on task	Off task	Loses focus frequently	Focuses on the task most of the time	Consistently stays on task
Uses time wisely	Does not work on task	Frequently gets off task	Most of the time works hard	Works hard and applies self to task
Works with the group	Unable to work in a group; disruptive or does not participate	Able to work with selected individuals	Works productively with others	Supports others and assumes a leadership role
Takes care of the materials	Disregards materials	Most of the materials are not picked up or taken care of	Leaves a few materials out	Picks up all materials and returns them to their proper places
Does the best work	Sloppy, disorganized, with numerous errors	Needs some help with content and/or errors	Good work with few mistakes and general information provided	Excellent work with no mistakes and solid content
Content	Student does not have an understanding of knowledge and skills related to the topic	Student has missing pieces related to skills and knowledge of the topic	Student has a good understanding of the skills and knowledge of the topic	Student has mastered the skills and knowledge of unit

Note. Task rubric. Sally Walker, 2010. Used with permission.

Some students may misbehave or act out, because they do not understand the content or because they already know the information and are bored. Another cause of misbehavior is that students do not understand the instructions. They need to see the instructions modeled, not just repeated, in order to understand what they are expected to do. Having a "go to" person can help free teacher time. The "go to" person can help with explaining expectations, and the job can rotate so that it is not the sole responsibility of one child to be the "go to" person. Misbehavior can also be a result of a student who is manipulating the situation. This child may know the material and be acting out because the curriculum is redundant for him.

If you identify the cause of misbehavior, it could lead to a recommendation for Tier 2 intervention on either end of the continuum or suggest more drastic curriculum differentiation in Tier 1.

For the Response to Intelligence Model™ to work, it is essential that the teacher knows the students well and establishes ongoing communications with them. What is going well? What do you feel uncertain about? What is working for you? What do you need help with? How does this fit with ___ (the topic)? What are you interested in? Can you make some connections with your topic to students' interests?

Curriculum

Another key to this model is *teaching to the top*. See all students as capable of learning and worthy of high-quality curriculum with respectful tasks. Select rich, engaging curriculum for all. Differentiation with boring tasks just leads to more boredom. Teaching facts so that students may do well on a test does not provide life skills or memorable, usable learning. Every level needs to have appealing, engaging, and respectful tasks that focus on essential knowledge and skills. High expectations need to be set with differentiation and scaffolding to lift all students instead of starting with grade-level curriculum and dumbing down the expectations. Teach up with high expectations and global content (concept based) that incorporate the big idea. Include essential questions and the skills to proceed with understanding of how the content makes sense of their world and how it relates to their lives. This makes the facts memorable, retainable, and usable rather than isolated and forgotten.

Global, concept-based, curriculum is structured to provide the whole picture, not just the pieces or facts. It is based on themes or concepts that reflect the whole picture. Knowledge is structured from the *big* picture, the concept, and then to the topic (what is important to know in the discipline) and moves to the facts (what must I know about this topic to be well informed and be able to function). All must be age appropriate.

The problem that exists in many classrooms is that teachers feel compelled to cover factual material for "the test." Students are learning isolated facts that have no relevance and rob them of the time to think above and beyond the facts or to apply what they know to problem solve. Students do not see connections between and among disciplines or are not exposed to the big ideas that cross over cultures or extend over time. In order that learning occurs on a grand scale, students must be engaged, not lectured, with content that is related to key concepts that frame the discipline, rather than a file of facts and a weak grasp of key concepts.

Examples of concepts and related topics include, but are not limited to:

Concept	Related Topics
Patterns	Weather, words and spelling, seasons, societies, mathematics, music, art
Conflict	Societies, peer conflict, gangs, wars, governance
Identity	Cultural diversity, personal identity
Structure	Poetry, societies, architecture, writing, music composition, art form
Change	Chemistry, medicine, technology, growth, vocabulary, communication, transportation
Trends	Clothing, food, medicine, transportation, communication

Note. Concept and Related Topics table. Sally Walker, 2010. Used with permission.

Beginning with the concept is responding to the need of the student to see the whole picture and opens multiple avenues to explore when designing intervention tiers. It provides the map with the possible places to go.

A question that arises is, "How does this relate to the standards?" The standards are not to be ignored; they must be woven into the framework. Most state standards are not concept-based but are based on what is believed to be essential content and skills. Often these are written in an objective format. The national science standards, however, are an example of a model that provides global concepts, with conceptual understandings based on critical content.

National Science Standards example (National Academy Press, 2000):

As a result of activities in grades K–12, all students should develop:
- Abilities necessary to do scientific inquiry, and
- Understandings about scientific inquiry.

Fundamental Understandings about Scientific Inquiry Grades K–4:

- Scientific investigations involve asking and answering a question and comparing the answer with what scientists already know about the world;
- Scientists use different kinds of investigations depending on the questions they are trying to answer;
- Simple instruments, such as magnifiers, thermometers, and rulers provide more information than scientists obtain using only their senses;
- Scientists develop explanations using observations (evidence) and what they already know about the world (scientific knowledge);
- Scientists make the results of their investigations public; they describe the investigations in ways that enable others to repeat the investigations; and
- Scientists review and ask questions about the results of other scientists' work.

If we are to look at the framework of curriculum, it might resemble Figure 4.2:

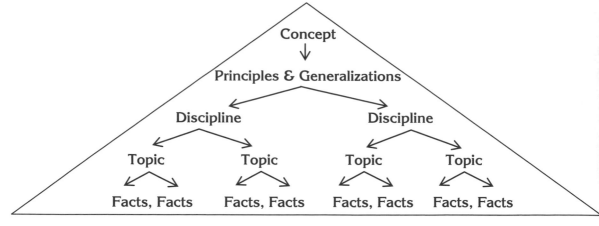

Figure 4.2. Curriculum framework.

What might the steps to a **Response to Intelligence** curriculum look like?

1. Introduce the concept with principles and generalizations.
2. Relate the concept to discipline(s) or interdisciplinary connections.
3. Specify the topic of study as key to understanding the discipline.
4. Introduce the topic with a hook or involvement in the topic.
5. Target the skill, knowledge, or behavior essential to the topic. Pre-assess understanding and knowledge of the topic.
6. Work with the topic to make decisions based on assessment data. Are interventions required?
7. Modify the curriculum to select and implement interventions.
8. Re-evaluate the tiers of interventions through formative assessments. Continue interventions, modify interventions, move students to the next tier, or refer students for additional special services.
9. Prepare on-going assessments and movement of grouping when needed.
10. Give final assessment.

Left 3	Left 2	1	Right 2	Right 3
Few key examples of content	Basic content	Core topic determined by district curriculum; state standards with applications and differentiation as needed by students	Differentiated; extended content	Extension activities that go beyond grade level with research or problem solving

The idea that teachers need to accommodate and build curriculum on students' diverse learning needs is far from new. Exceptional learning needs require some kind of adaptation on both ends of the learning continuum. For giftedness to flourish it must be nurtured. Special education has known and responded to this notion for some time. Special education emphasizes flexibility, continuous dynamic assessment, and flexible programming.

Appropriate curriculum for gifted learners may emphasize the content focusing on learning the skills and concepts within a body of knowledge. Acceleration through the content area is recommended. Another way to view curriculum for gifted students is to focus on the concept looking at themes, principles, or ideas that go across disciplines or domains of knowledge. The teacher in this view is the questioner who raises ideas or issues for discussion or debate. A third way to approach curriculum for gifted students is through higher level questioning. Within this curriculum, the process and product are highlighted through skills of investigation and problem solving. This differs from the content model in that the content is more incidental and the skill development and products are heightened (VanTassel-Baska & Stambaugh, 2005).

There are many books published that provide opportunities for effective differentiation for gifted students. Kingore's (2004) *Differentiation: Simplified, Realistic and Effective; How to Challenge Advanced Potentials in Mixed-Ability Classrooms* provides many teacher-friendly activities to support classroom differentiation and includes reproducible activities and an interactive CD-Rom. Coil's *Successful Teaching in the Differentiated Classroom* (2007) and *Activities and Assessments for the Differentiated Classroom* (2004) present comprehensive, practical, easy-to-implement strategies with reproducibles and CDs. These publications are excellent additions to the teacher's toolbox and provide appropriate challenge to gifted students.

Affective Differentiation

In the same way that academic differentiation is required, so is affective differentiation sorely needed. The model works well for this area also. Most children do well and thrive in the basic classroom environment. Students are supported in their work, feel good about themselves and their work, and respond to personal situations appropriately. When behavior becomes inappropriate they may be relocated to Tier 2 where the school counselor or social worker meets with them in small groups to guide them through a difficult period or time in their lives, to help them work through a situation, or to give them coping tools to manage behavior. Tier 3 requires individualized help with a counselor or social worker and may involve family counseling as well.

It is important in this model that students come to recognize that we all have differences. Differences are what make us who we are; they make us unique. What may be appropriate for one learner is not always appropriate for another. What is easy for me may be difficult for you. What may be a snap for you to do, may cause me to struggle. Support of each learner is essential, rather than competition with each other. This is a cooperative, not competitive, model.

Not only is it important for learners to achieve academically, but it is also important to have skills and attitudes that allow for the effective processing of information and to possess the skills to interact with others in a socially acceptable manner. Affective areas that may present problems where interventions are needed for students may include, but are not limited to:

- underachievement;
- fear of failure;
- perfectionism;
- negative peer pressure;
- self-concept, self-confidence, self-esteem;
- lack of self-understanding concerning learning style;
- identifying and management of emotions and behavior;
- self-control, self-discipline, self-management;
- conflict management;
- recognition of consequences;
- decision making;
- problem solving;
- identification of personal qualities and external supports;
- setting and achieving goals;
- recognition of feelings and perspectives of others;
- use of communication skills to effectively interact with others; and
- contribution to the well being of others and society.

Interventions can range from moving the student's desk location to the changing of classrooms. It may mean having a series of talks with parents, the teacher, counselor/social worker, or administrator. Some interventions may include but are not limited to:

- working with a mentor;
- becoming a mentor;
- assigning a "buddy" helper,
- interest group that shares a passion or concern;
- completing a planning task sheet for the day (half day or hour) as needed;
- bibliotherapy;
- schedule change,
- time away from others, quiet time,;

- time to exercise, run laps, or shoot baskets to release excess energy;
- meetings with parents/ guardians;
- frequent phone calls or notes to parents/guardians;
- diet change;
- journaling;
- meeting with social worker;
- small group discussions or work;
- becoming a group leader;
- finding a role model (hero or shero);
- discovering an outlet for emotions: music, art, dance, writing, and drama;
- community service assignment;
- exploring future choices or careers and steps needed to achieve;
- detention; and
- change of school.

The Mindset of the Teacher Is Crucial

The Response to Intelligence Model™ symbolizes that all are capable of learning and that teaching is recognizing and providing for the differences within and among students in order to provide growth for all. Each student has a right to grow. As a teacher, you have no control over what you start with; you can only control what you do (or may not do) with whatever it is the students bring with them. This is about knowing your students and providing opportunities for them to grow as learners.

Sitting down and chatting with the students on a one-to-one basis helps immensely and pays off in gold. Letting students know you see them as an individual is crucial. It says, "You are important to me. I value and believe in you." The teacher-student connection helps the teacher plan what to do with the student, what interventions may be appropriate, and sets the stage for effective differentiation. Students are more motivated as they learn that their teacher cares about and believes in them. The teacher-student connection also builds a positive mind set with a community of learners who believe in and support each other.

ᏕᏉᏣ

*"Until every gifted child can attend a school
where the brightest are appropriately challenged
in an environment with their intellectual peers,
America can't claim that
it's leaving no child behind."*

Jan and Bob Davidson
Genius Denied

REFERENCES

Batsche, G., Elliott, J., Graden, J. L., Grimes, J., Kovaleski, J. F., Prasse, D., et al., (2005). National Association of State Directors of Special Education, Inc.

Response to intervention: Policy considerations and implementation. Presented to the Illinois State Board of Education (ISBE) and incorporated into the Illinois State Response to Intervention (RtI) Plan, January 1, 2008. Springfield, IL: ISBE. Retrieved from http://www.isbe.net/pd/rti_state_plan.pdf

Coil, C. (2009). *Differentiation, RTI, and achievement: How they work together.* Marion, IL: Pieces of Learning.

Coleman, M. R,. & Hughes, C. E. (2009). Meeting the needs of gifted students within an RtI framework. *Gifted Child Today, 32*(3), 14-17.

Medina, J. (2009, November). *Gifted education integrated in RtI instruction systems.* Paper presented at the annual meeting of the National Association for Gifted Children, St. Louis, MO.

National Academy Press, (2000). *Inquiry and the National Science Education standards: A guide for teaching and learning.* Washington, D.C.: Center for Science, Mathematics, and Engineering Education.

Tomlinson, C. (1999). *The differentiated classroom: Responding to the needs of all learners.* Alexandria, VA: Association for Supervision and Curriculum Development .

VanTassel-Baska, J., & Stambaugh, T. (2005). *Comprehensive curriculum for gifted learners* (3rd ed.). Needham Heights, MA: Allyn and Bacon.

Chapter 5

How Does the Development of Creativity Support the NEW RtI?

Creativity, according to Barbara Clark (Clark, 2005, p. 64) is "the highest form of giftedness." Whether a child is termed accelerated, a high-achiever, or even "gifted," the development of creativity is essential to the high-end learner. Creativity belongs in all tiers of the NEW RtI but is essential in Right Tier 2 and Right Tier 3 for develop-ment of gifted potential.

We have seen in earlier chapters that creativity is part of most definitions of gif-tedness. The U.S.D.O.E. includes creative high performance capability in its 1972 definition originally defined in the Marland report. This multiple talent definition of gifts and talents includes creativity, leadership, and the arts and focuses on demon-strated or potential abilities. Note that it also includes underachievers, a group of students with high potential who may not demonstrate high performance. Undera-chievers are often highly creative.

Known as the "Father of Creativity," E. Paul Torrance (1915-2003) has contri-buted much of our understanding of creativity and its relation to giftedness. In his nearly 60 years of research, he set out to create and validate measures to identify creative potential. Out of this commitment came the Torrance Tests of Creative Thinking (TTCT) which arguably quantifies both identification and the development of creativity. He helped disprove the theory that IQ tests alone are sufficient to identi-fy intelligence. He also felt confident that creativity can not only be identified but in-creased through practice. Torrance also created the Future Problem Solving Pro-gram that focuses on creative thinking and is included as part of many gifted pro-grams. He was concerned about the decline in creativity in the United States and developed classroom activities to challenge students to think creatively about the future.

His increased awareness of the importance of the development of creativity led to the development of the TTCT which is the most popular identifier of creativity in this country. The test is administered through a choice of two formats: Verbal and Figural. The verbal test involves uses for common objects. The figural test, recognized as more free from cultural bias, is appropriate for the kindergarten level through graduate school. Students respond by taking simple shapes and adding details to create more complete pictures. Responses are evaluated for fluency (number of ideas), flexibility (number of category changes), originality (the statistically infrequent response), and elaboration (idea details). These categories can be included as part of gifted program services to enhance creativity. These tests are perhaps the best-known and highly reputed battery of divergent thinking. They have been used in over 2000 studies and have been translated into more than 32 languages.

The work of E. Paul Torrance is foundational to our understanding of creativity. On the other hand, a creativity test is not always available to classroom teachers. How can creativity also be recognized using observable characteristics in the classroom?

On the next page is a list of creative characteristics as created by Joan Smutny, Director, Center for Gifted, National-Louis University.

Characteristics of Highly Creative Children

The highly creative child:

1. reacts positively to new, strange, or mysterious elements in his/her environment;
2. is curious, investigative; asks penetrating questions;
3. is imaginative, creates fantasies, tells stories;
4. is full of ideas, fluent;
5. has a strong and persistent sense of humor;
6. is emotionally responsive, often empathetic;
7. likes to play with ideas;
8. shows a sense of wonder; a heightened awareness of the world;
9. tends to daydream;
10. has a great deal of energy;
11. is spontaneous, impulsive, uninhibited;
12. tends to resist authority;
13. is independent, individualistic, self-sufficient;
14. is sensitive to beauty, nature, animals;
15. feels strongly about many things; has a strong sense of justice;
16. experiments with whatever is at hand; improvises;
17. is an intuitive thinker;
18. sees relationships among seemingly unrelated ideas;
19. is usually socially accepted by peers; and
20. shows strength of will, which may appear rigid or stubborn
(J. Smutny, personal communication, 2009).

One of the most important / influential contributors to the field of gifted education, Dr. Joseph Renzulli, determined that truly gifted and talented persons who make significant contributions to society have three characteristics (Renzulli & Reis, 2008). They have above average ability, strong task commitment, and high levels of creativity. Each area is a part of formal identification of these students for gifted services, and it is further felt that motivation and creativity are developmental objectives for these children.

Renzulli and Reis (2008) have created one of the best-known curriculum models for gifted that includes high levels of creativity development: The Enrichment Triad Model. This model is appropriate for any content area and grade level in multiple grouping arrangements. It is also very appropriate for any RtI intervention because it consists of three levels or stages of enrichment. Type I (General Exploratory Activities) enrichment is appropriate for Tier 1 students. An example would be exploring topics that are not a part of the regular school curriculum and materials would be available from a resource center or through field trips. ALL students could benefit from these activities.

Type II enrichment (Group Training Activities) has the purpose of developing skills in cognitive and affective thinking, learning skills, advanced research skills, and written, oral, and visual communication skills. These activities are appropriate for small groups where specific focus and challenge are appropriate for these students. Type II is more appropriate for Right Tier 2 students, although some Tier I students could benefit depending on areas of readiness and interests.

Type III enrichment (Individual and Small Group investigations) is specifically for those students who can benefit from intense in-depth explorations of real problems in any area–arts, sciences, etc. These investigations result in a product and are presented to an audience. In RtI, this type of enrichment is perfect for Right Tier 3. It should be noted that Renzulli envisioned this model incorporated into a Schoolwide Enrichment Model in which all students participate.

Other traditional models that encourage creative thinking include the Feldhusen Three-Stage Model (1980)–basic divergent and convergent thinking, complex creative and problem-solving activities, and independent learning, Dr. Calvin Taylor's Multiple-Talent Totem Pole Model (1978), Betts' Autonomous Learner Model (1999), Schlichter's Talents Unlimited (1986), and Cox, Daniel, and Boston's Pyramid Model (1985). All are appropriate for advanced students and provide appropriate challenge whether they are placed in Tiers 1, 2, or 3.

The Parallel Curriculum (PCM) is a recent curriculum design created to develop and challenge high-ability learners at increasing levels of intellectual demand using both critical and creative thinking (Tomlinson, et. al., 2002). It takes the regular or core curriculum within any discipline (facts, concepts, principles, and skills) and provides appropriate challenge and pacing. Students apply knowledge using the tools of experts in a given content field, are given opportunities to learn about relationships across other disciplines, and are provided opportunities to develop an understanding within and across disciplines (curriculum of connections). Students are also encouraged to develop curiosity, pursue topics that are of interest to them, find questions that appeal to them, and learn the skills used by professionals in the field with the curriculum of practice. The practice parallel guides students as questioners, problem solvers, or researchers to explore and examine how professionals in the field work. Creativity is needed for each of these areas.

In addition, the parallel of identity has the student examine: *What is intriguing to me? How do I cope, respond when faced with difficulties? How do I handle things when there is ambiguity, uncertainty, failure, success, compromise, and competition? How am I affected? How am I shaped?* Setting goals for self along with self-introspection requires a high level of creative thinking. Assessment of prior knowledge is essential and ensures that students are working at their challenge level. This model is supported by NAGC and is highly appropriate for those students in Right Tier 2 and Right Tier 3. Finally, it is not necessary to use this model in its entirety. The use of any part of this model will provide appropriate challenge for high-end learners.

It is important to realize that creativity should be at the center of education for these students. There are tests that are available to assess creativity, and activities to develop it. By far the most-used creativity tests are the Torrance Tests of Creative Thinking. They are available in several formats, and there are multiple programs and activities available to develop creative areas such as fluency, flexibility, originality, and elaboration. Although these tests took ten years to develop, have a strong history of validation, and have both figural and verbal versions, some feel that too many creatively gifted children are missed using these measures. These tests should never be used to determine that a child is NOT creative but only to indicate when a child demonstrates potential. Identifying the creative individual is challenging, indeed.

There are methods that are used in schools and businesses to enhance creative thinking. One of the best methods is brainstorming (Davis, 2004). Developed by Dr. Alex Osborn in 1963, there are four rules to brainstorming:

1. No criticism,
2. Crazy off-the-wall ideas are encouraged,
3. Combining ideas together to form new ones (sometimes called piggy-backing or hitchhiking) are desired, and
4. Quantities of ideas are desired.

Examples of creative thinking techniques include:

*   Brainstorming: "List all of the ideas you can think of to . . ."
*   Reverse brainstorming: "How many ways can we think of not to . . ."
*   Analogical thinking: "How is a key like a painting?"
*   Visualization: "Imagine a place you would like to visit but have never been there."
*   What would happen if . . . "oil were discovered in your town?"

There are also wonderful programs committed to developing and using creativity such as the Future Problem Solving Bowl (that developed out of the Creative Problem Solving Model), Destination Imagination, and Odyssey of the Mind (among many others).

The most important focus should be on appropriate depth and complexity. This will provide challenge and growth for students who spend most of their day in a traditional, age-appropriate curriculum that doesn't normally give them the opportunity to develop skills and abilities to help them be successful in their own lives–including struggle with challenging and demanding material.

The development of creativity is essential to any RtI program.

The Use of Drama to Enhance Creativity and Challenge Gifted Students in Tier 1 and Right Tier 2 Activities

So how can the creative gifted child be motivated and challenged? Daniel H. Pink has called for a shift in education to right-brained thinking in order to prepare students for their future (Pink, 2006). Essential to this preparation is visual, whole-brain thinking including creativity and higher order thinking skills. His six senses of high concept and high-touch focus on story, synthesis, empathy, and play with a concentration on making meaning and purpose in life. These concepts are seldom taught in schools, yet they are a perfect challenge for the creatively gifted child.

An important instructional technique sometimes called process drama, or drama-in-education is one tool that should be part of every teacher's toolbox. Process drama is an instructional technique based on the combination of student-based inquiry using dramatic techniques.

It evolved (and continues to evolve) from the principles of creative drama, also known as creative dramatics, and drama-in-education. It was developed in the United Kingdom and Canada by Dorothy Heathcote and Gavin Bolton for the purpose of deeper student understanding of complex educational concepts. This model has been included as part of pre-service teacher training in the U.K., Canada, and Australia.

The focus is on student inquiry, critical thinking, creative thinking, and problem solving. Students and teachers create and explore an imaginary world together to discover skills and create deeper learning into a given topic. It begins when the teacher/facilitator creates a framework, or drama structure, for students to explore through improvisation.

Elements:

- consists of a series of activities that take place over a longer period of time;
- begins with a scenario that establishes setting, roles, focus, and atmosphere;
- deals with concepts to be explored;
- builds on inquiry, issues, events, and relationships;
- focuses on acquiring new knowledge through active participation;
- requires all participants to adopt roles and interact with each other;
- self-reflection and assessment are essential to the process;
- it is experienced, not performed for others; and
- the teacher becomes a facilitator to "guide from the side."

Process drama has many published materials, many through Heinemann Publishing, that will guide the teacher in the exploration of this valuable instructional classroom technique. A good resource is the excellent (and free) site at http://www.creativedrama.org. It gives a clear definition of process drama and provides sample lessons and ideas for the teacher to use in the classroom. An example of this drama structure (O'Neill, Lambert, Linnell, & Warr-Wood, 1977) is on the following page.

VOLCANOES

A drama for Grades 3 and 4
Adapted by Penny Choice from the drama structure Volcanoes (O'Neill et al., 1977)
for use with gifted elementary learners in the regular classroom

The teacher talks at some length to students to discover the extent of their knowledge about volcanoes. The students are then divided into differentiated groups to learn more about volcanoes. Each group reads one of the books and reports back to the entire group. Books in order of difficulty (from struggling learners to gifted) include:

Chevat, R. (2002). *Volcano Diary: Mount Saint Helens.* New York, NY : McGraw-Hill School
    Division.
Halpern, M. (2002). *Volcanoes.* Washington D.C.: National Geographic Society.
Gaskins, P. (2002). *Look out for lava.* Orlando, FL: Harcourt.
Lauber, P. (1986). *Volcano: The eruption and healing of Mount St. Helens.* New York, NY:
    Scholastic.
And for ELL (Spanish) language students:
Argueta, M. (1990). *Magic Dogs of the Volcanoes* (in English and Spanish). Marina, CA:
    Children's Book Press.

Then the teacher asks students if they would like to create a story about volcanoes so they can understand what it felt like when the volcano erupted. She explains that she will start the story that takes place on an island long ago, and the students will find clues in what she says that will help them decide who in the story they are and what has happened. She begins by describing the island and the volcano that has always been part of the people's lives and then stops to make sure students are involved in the story. *Who are they? What is happening here?* The teacher then moves away from them and returns to the group as the leader.

"I have just been to look at the damage of the volcano—but the village is gone. The volcano has destroyed it. We are all safe on this hillside. What are we to do?"

"Did anyone manage to save anything?" The teacher prompts with suggestions only as needed. "Food? belongings?" The group decides to pool their food and belongings, and they arrange to put someone in charge of the food, etc. The group then shares their first meal on the hillside. (Any inconsistencies or incongruities are gently worked into the story as carefully as possible.)

After they have eaten, the teacher asks them what they are going to do for shelter for the night. It is beginning to get dark and will begin to get colder during the night. "Where shall you seek shelter?" As they settle down for the night, the teacher asks the following questions: "What shall you do tomorrow? Do you want to stay together? Do you want to rebuild the village? What will you build your houses of? What about fresh water? Food? Do you want to farm the land? What will be involved? How will you get tools to do what you need?"

This can go on to a second session to develop the story further or can be concluded here with the teacher telling in story form what has taken place during the play about volcanoes.

Further activities might include:

- journaling/diary about experiences,

- *tableaux* (stage pictures) about events,

- scenes heightening and deepening the drama,

- creating pictures/drawings about the eruption and following or drawing the new village,

- drawing the rebirth of the land and its wildlife after the eruption, and

- students are now grandparents many years later telling their stories to their own grandchildren.

Assessment: Drama participation assessment

- writing and journaling, concept mapping about volcanoes; or

- paper and pencil test if desired based on state standards (science, social studies, language arts, fine arts).

It is also important to teach this unit at a high conceptual level. One way of in-suring that the depth and complexity is appropriate for gifted learners is to deter-mine what students should know, understand, and do during the unit. Therefore, students will:

Know: The history and geography of volcanoes

Volcano vocabulary

Requirements of state standards

Understand: Events have an influence over our choices

Volcanoes significantly affect the geology of the earth

Environmental change affects the social and economic structure of a culture

Do: Research the history of volcanoes

Participate in the development of the drama with enthusiasm and cooperation

Work collaboratively in groups

There are many examples of published drama structures written by a variety of authors for teachers to use in their own classrooms. From O'Neill and Lambert's *Haunted House* (1977) which focuses on developing mystery stories to their *The Way West* (1982) which helps students understand the hardships suffered on the Oregon Trail by interacting with the experiences on the trip the diversity of drama is explored at a deep and complex level.

Penny Choice developed an example of a Right Tier 2 activity for small groups of gifted students in 2002. Highlights of *The Silk Road Project* are on the following page.

The Silk Road Project

A middle level drama strategy adapted from various resources by Penny Choice

Essential Questions:

- What happens when strangers meet?

- Why is it important to bring different cultures together?

- How do ideas travel?

- Why are the arts essential?

- Why is it important for Americans to understand the contributions of the Silk Road?

Mantle of the Expert (a technique developed by Dorothy Heathcote): Students are Ethnographers from the Smithsonian Center for Folklife and Cultural Heritage. In their study of races and cultures of mankind, they are assembled to learn about the contributions of the Silk Road to society today. They are collaborating with famous cellist, Yo Yo Ma, and his Silk Road Ensemble to further the cause of fostering creativity through cultural exchange. They are preparing an article for the *Smithsonian* magazine.

Highlights include:

- artifacts display and music experience from Yo Yo Ma;

- ongoing research;

- process drama takes place in ancient china (200 c. e.);

- group agrees to travel together;

- essential questions are researched and discussed;

- caravan is outfitted: their personal camel is bought and named,

- experience the trip: dangers; communicating with other cultures;

- crossing the Taklamakan Desert and the Tianshan Mountains;

- a stop at the ruined city of Niya;

- Samarkand: what happens when strangers meet;

- celebration and a separation; and

- return home.

Finally, the teacher says, "Generation after generation, in each family, the story of their travels was handed down, orally, sometimes in art, sometimes drawn, according to the interests of each. It is today, and, in pairs or threes, the older generation telling the story of the Silk Road travels to the younger generation. Tell the story as you remember it."

The ethnographers from the *Smithsonian* meet and prepare their article for the magazine. They discuss the answers to the essential questions and the enduring understandings. They write/draw/create the article. They then assess their work.

This unit took about six weeks in meetings during gifted language arts period for 45 minutes a day, once or twice a week.

Students who are encouraged to be creative keep their creativity far beyond the school setting. The use of process drama helps insure the development of higher level thinking demanded for success in the 21st Century.

REFERENCES

Betts, G., & Kercher, J. J. (1999). *Autonomous learner model: Optimizing ability.* Greeley, CO: ALPS Publishing.

Clark, B. (2005). *Growing up gifted* (5th ed.). Upper Saddle River, NJ: Pearson.

Cox, J., Daniel, N., & Boston, B. O. (1985). *Educating able learners: Programs and promising practices.* Austin, TX: University of Texas Press.

Davis, G. A. (2004). *Creativity is forever* (5th ed.). Dubuque, IA: Kendall/Hunt.

Feldhusen, J. (1980). *The three-state model of course design.* Englewood Cliffs, NJ: Educational Technology Publications.

O'Neill, C., & Lambert, A., (1982). *Drama structures.* London, England: Hutchinson.

O'Neill, C., Lambert, A., Linnell, R., & Warr-Wood, J. (1977). *Drama guidelines.* Portsmouth, NH: Heinemann.

Pink, D. H. (2006). *A whole new mind: Why right brainers will rule the world.* New York, NY: Penguin.

Renzulli, J., & Reis, S. (2008). *Enriching curriculum for all students* (2nd ed.). Thousands Oaks, CA: Corwin Press.

Schlichter, C. L. (1986). Talents unlimited: An inservice education model for teaching thinking skills. *Gifted Child Quarterly, 30,* 119-123.

Taylor, C. W. (1978). How many types of giftedness can you program tolerate? *Journal of Creative Behavior, 12,* 39-51.

Tomlinson, C. A., Kaplan, S. N., Renzulli, S. J., Purcell, J., Leppien, J., & Burns, D. (2002). *The parallel curriculum: A design to develop high potential and challenge high-ability learners.* Thousand Oaks, CA: Corwin.

Chapter 6

Advocacy

How do I have my voice heard?

What is needed to assure success for the gifted population?

"What can I do when my child is not learning? How do I even begin to approach the school?" asks a concerned parent of a gifted child. "My child is bored, feels that school is a waste of time, and is creating excuses to not go to school."

This scenario happens more frequently than it should, and parents of a gifted child may have to face the situation one or more times during their child's schooling. Some parents are fearful of speaking out, afraid that they will be regarded as one of *those* pushy parents. Teachers, whose plates are already spilling over with responsibilities, are not necessarily looking to take on even more work. They are overwhelmed by the many needs of their students and the difficult task of reaching and teaching all students. Some may even perceive that nothing is wrong because the gifted child is getting an **A** and is at or above grade level. It is believed that there *is* no problem. Why fix something that is going well, as they perceive it?

Our gifted and talented children deserve an appropriate education that does not leave them behind. They deserve to learn something new every day (just like their age peers do), and to have the opportunity to struggle with challenging content, not to serve as the unpaid teacher helping other students or to be bored by relearning material that was learned previously.

Misconceptions surround gifted education and gifted children. Sympathies do not abound for the gifted and talented child, their teacher(s), or their parent(s). One of the most erroneous misconceptions that continues to exist is that the gifted and talented child does not need help. Because he is gifted, he does not need extra assistance and support. He can make it on his own. We must continue to dispel this misunderstanding.

All gifted children do not necessarily make it on their own. They need parental support, teachers who understand them, and challenging curriculum with the appropriate depth, complexity, and pacing to challenge and enrich learning. The Marland Report in 1972 found that if not challenged, many young gifted children decide whether they will use their gifts or adapt to regular classroom expectations by fourth grade. A kindergarten girl who was reading voraciously at home was sitting quietly in her class going through basic pre-reading instruction. When asked if her teacher knew she could read, she responded, "No, I don't want the other kids to feel bad because they can't read. I don't want to be different." She was already adapting to classroom expectations that did not recognize and provide for anyone beyond the norm in kindergarten. In her district, a child cannot be identified as gifted until grade four.

Gifted students are the most underachieving students in the classroom. When comparing their potential with their achievement levels huge gaps exist. Parents and teachers may wrongly assume that because a student got an A or is at the top of her class that there is no underachievement. But, a problem exists in that an **A** may mean she had previously mastered the content and that she may not have learned anything new. The gifted child may waste time reiterating what she has already learned. She may, however, lack study skills or the ability to tackle new complex information. Sometimes gifted students must wait to get to college to grapple with difficult material. Other times even college may not be challenging. These students need exposure to problem solving, research, and/or concept-based curriculum that delves into the study of the discipline and all that is involved. Gifted students need an equal opportunity to learn. If they are left behind, our society loses.

Other misconceptions also surround gifted education and promote the notion that gifted children do not need the specialized help and support that children with learning difficulties receive. One such misconception is that gifted children are easy to teach. However, they are as diverse in nature as any group could possibly be.

Within a classroom of students, you may have a student who is a resident expert in math. This student could blow the top off math charts for his age, yet he may not care about reading. His language arts and reading scores may even be below grade level. He is not interested in reading and does not want to be bothered by anything but his love–advanced math. Similarly, we may have a student who has been reading since age three, who writes beautifully, and is constantly immersed in literature. She could care less about math. It is not her cup of tea! Both are in the same class. Both have special needs that are as diverse from the average child as the child with learning disabilities, yet many states do not require any special courses or training for the teachers of gifted students. Most colleges and universities do not have courses in their teacher training curricula that include recognizing and programming for the characteristics and needs of gifted students.

Educators need training in recognizing and identifying the varieties of gifted students and learning how to meet their diverse needs. Part of meeting their needs includes becoming an advocate for them.

Who is customarily not recognized is the student who is getting straight **A**'s and may be the one in class learning the least. The gifted learner may have already mastered the material years earlier and may just be reiterating information already learned. There is no new learning. No challenge is occurring. The difficulty with this situation is that the learner may adopt the mode of thinking that all learning should be effortless.

Part of the problem in dealing with gifted children is that they are such a diverse population. They have an excess of ability rather than a deficit. Their excess of ability may be general intellectual (good across all academic areas) or in a particular specialized area. One might be good in reading, but may lack in another academic area. Another child might be gifted in music. Yet another student may be enthralled with history or science. And if not given the opportunity to be involved in experiences that showcase other talents, their gifts may not be identified in the traditional classroom. Still another child might have creativity that leads to new ideas, off beat answers, and a different view of the world. Like Calvin in *Calvin and Hobbs*, this child asks "why?" sees things beyond the realm of the classroom, and thinks outside of the box. The creatively gifted child marches to the beat of his own drummer and may not do well on tests.

Research has shown that parents are better at identifying gifted students than are teachers without training (Chia, Harris, Hoffman, & Potter, 1974). Those teachers tend to identify teacher pleasers or high academic achievers rather than the truly gifted students. Part of this may be due to the fact that some gifted students may not have timing and tact that leads to politeness and manners. Gifted students may, in fact, be upset with the school for their lack of appropriate programming, and they do not suffer fools gladly. Unfortunately this only perpetuates the myth that gifted are an elitist population.

Relative to Response to Intelligence, gifted education representatives need to be at the table when RtI is being discussed. The learner may not have a clue how to manage time or how to chunk long-term assignments into bite-size pieces. When that learner reaches a point where learning is difficult, that student may not know how to cope. He may give up without trying or feel that he is really an imposter after all. ALL students have the right to learn something new every day and to experience challenge with content that has depth and complexity and is at a different pace than the traditional curriculum. Others in the school, campus, or district must be aware that for growth to occur in ALL students we cannot neglect those children at the top who already know the content and can do the work. The Response to Intelligence Model™ applies to gifted children as much as it does to special needs children. Committee members must realize and accept that differentiation is not reserved solely for those students who are struggling at the left of Tier 1.

In order for challenge to occur, parents and teachers need to advocate for the gifted student. Create a portfolio to start the process. Begin with documenting what the student knows or does that is above grade-level expectations. Save examples of the student's exemplary work or work that demonstrates growth over time. When beginning new learning save a copy of beginning work and then work on the same specific content a few days, weeks, or months later. Compare the beginning work with the later piece. This gives examples of growth over time. List books that the child has read, questions the child has asked, vocabulary words that are extraordinary, or math problems that the child has solved. Take pictures of projects done, record problems solved, describe experiments the child has designed, etc. Be sure to date all the work. This evidence of work will help the school program for the learner's strengths.

We are in an age of accountability where we need proof that students have done the work or mastered the concept. The more documentation you have the easier it is to plead your case. Note: Be sure that it is work done by the student and NOT an adult!

Secondly, meet with people who can effect change. In most cases for the parent, this will be the child's teacher(s). If you are a teacher who wants something different for the child, meet with the team that may be working with the child. Be sure to include the gifted program coordinator, if there is one, and the principal. You will need support from the school administration if change is to occur.

In meetings begin with something positive before launching into complaints or demanding what you want to happen. A positive attitude of wanting to help others on the team do their best rather than threatening, blaming, or demeaning current practices strengthens your cause. Be prepared to defend and justify what you want to happen and have documentation you need to support that change. Be aware that it may take baby steps to get the change. Take one step at a time, and recognize the teacher and/or school's effort when it occurs–no matter how small it is.

Volunteer to help when that is possible. Schools today have extremely tight budgets and extra hands are welcome. Working in the school as a room helper, field trip chaperone, or library or office assistant helps you become familiar with the school, personnel, and practices. This does not mean that you will necessarily be working with your child or even in his classroom. You are working as part of a team to build the school, not a destructive force to tear it down. Suggestions and changes are more readily accepted from you when you are working with the system as a change agent.

Many states do not have funding to support gifted education or any legislation to support teacher training in gifted education. Any gifted programming or professional development for the staff may be the responsibility of the local district. Districts have so many under-funded mandates that gifted programming may be an area that is hard to sell. For this reason, it is important that you advocate at the state level. Find out if you have state funds for gifted education. Is there a state mandate to support gifted programming or certification in gifted education for educators? What language is there in the school code to support gifted education statewide? If you do have state support, it will make working with your district considerably easier. If there is minimal or no state support find out why there is none. The state gifted affiliate organization may need your help to increase legislative awareness so that change at the state level can happen.

Find out who the state leaders are and how you can help. Some states are working on legislation and/or funding. Get to know what their goals are and what legislation may be pending. Visit with your legislators. Share your personal story, and ask them to support funding for gifted education. Democracy is all about relationships and getting your voice heard. Don't be afraid to speak up.

It is not surprising that most people feel intimidated when there is a need to contact state legislators. This is not something that advocates willingly choose to do. But, remember that this is the backbone of our government in the United States. We live in a country where we elect the people we want to represent us. The elected officials are there to be our voice. In order for them to know how to best represent us, we must communicate our needs to them. They need to hear our concerns and desires. One legislator commented that if he gets 10 calls it means he had better pay attention to the issue. Gifted education is an issue that needs attention!

Legislators respond better to brief statements. They have so many issues and much to read and digest. Be concise. Make it personal. Tell your story about your child or grandchild. Make your phone call. Write it out. Send a fax. Follow up by using the information in a letter. If the representative or senator is not available personally for a phone call, talk to his/her education aid. This is the person who has the legislator's ear. Many times this is the person who makes the decision and advises the legislator how to vote.

Get in touch with your gifted state affiliate organization and volunteer to help. Many state affiliates sponsor a gifted convention every year. This is an excellent way to meet other parents and teachers who are advocating and making a difference for gifted children. If you are able, donate a day at the convention to your child's teacher or another teacher in your district. Not only will your child benefit, but also so may others.

Another rich resource is NAGC. Their website http://www.nagc.org has a multitude of resources that can help you on your journey. NAGC also has a convention every year. The convention is held in different cities in the United States. If you are able, you will want to participate. Leaders in gifted education share their latest ideas, research, and best practices. It is truly motivating.

Federally there are few funds for gifted education. In fact, less than $.02 out of every $100 spent on education is designated for gifted students. Nationally the allocated gifted money goes to the Javits Grant which funds the National Research Center for Gifted housed at the University of Connecticut. Javits grants are allocated for researching issues that concern gifted and talented children. These funds are so small that they do not help support states. States are completely independent when it comes to gifted dollars.

It helps if you have others working with you. Numbers count! Are there other folks who feel the way that you do? Are there parents or teachers with similar concerns? What is your school board's position on gifted education? One parent was so upset with the decisions being made about the gifted program she ran for the school board and was elected. Most program decisions are made at the local level, and your voice can count and make a huge difference.

REFERENCES

Chia, R., Harris, C. R., Hoffman, C., & Potter, M. (1974). Parents as identifiers of giftedness, ignored but accurate. *Gifted Child Quarterly. 18,* 191-195.

Marland, S. P., Jr. (1972). *Education of the gifted and talented: Report to the Congress of the United States by the U.S. Commissioner of Education and background papers submitted to the U.S. Office of Education.* Washington, DC: U.S. Government Printing Office. (Government Documents Y4.L 11/2: G36)

"If you are continually asked to jump over a bar that requires little or no effort, how long will it be before you will not be able to jump any higher?"

Carol Ann Tomlinson

Interventions

Interventions look differently at various tiers. Interventions are also different whether they are for the students at the Left Tiers (struggling) or at the Right Tiers (advanced). However, there are some general suggestions and principles for any RtI design. In 2006, the Iowa Department of Education created general principles that apply to ALL students.

Iowa's Principles for RtI Design

- All students are part of one proactive educational system.
  All students can learn.
  Use all available resources to teach all students.
- Use scientific, research-based instruction.
  Curriculum and instructional approaches must have a high probability of success.
- Use instructional time efficiently and effectively.
- Use instructionally relevant assessments that are reliable and valid.
  Screening: Collect data for the purpose of identifying low- and high-performing students at risk for not having their needs met.
  Diagnostic: Gather information from multiple sources to determine why students are not benefiting from instruction.
  Formative: Collect frequent, ongoing information, including both formal and informal data, to guide instruction.
- Use a problem-solving method to make decisions based on a continuum of student needs.

Provide strong core classroom curriculum, instruction, and assessment.

Provide increasing levels of support based on increasing levels of student needs.

- Use data to guide instructional decisions.

Align curriculum and instruction to assessment data.

Allocate resources.

Drive professional-development decisions.

- Use professional development and follow-up modeling and coaching to ensure effective instruction at all levels.

Provide ongoing training and support to assimilate new knowledge and skills.

Anticipate and be willing to meet the newly emerging needs based on student performance.

- Leadership is vital.

Provide strong administrative support to ensure commitment and resources.

Provide strong teacher support to share in the common goal of improving instruction.

Allow a leadership team to build internal capacity and sustainability over time

(Allington, 2009).

Following are intervention highlights that apply to all classrooms:

- The "one-size-fits-all" curriculum plan is unacceptable in today's schools. The use of only grade-level materials is insufficient. Many students on both ends of the continuum are left behind. Today's schools need multi-level texts;

- The use of a single intervention design is not appropriate–especially the use of a single commercial product;

- Vocabulary knowledge varies widely. Schools must be aware of and address background vocabulary knowledge at all levels;

- The use of a 30-minute intervention is inappropriate and insufficient. Side-by-side teaching is essential for struggling students; mentorships are important to high-end students;

- Whole-group direct instruction should be used ONLY when the entire class needs specific information;

- Small-group instruction should be matched to the needs of the students;

- Ongoing assessment and feedback is essential;

- A match between the reader and the text level is part of Tiers 1, 2, and 3. Readability guides and decoding word rules will be different for each tier;

- All interventions should be coordinated with the core curriculum in the classroom;

- Teachers need to be or utilize experts in reading instruction. Note that the expertise differs for struggling and advanced readers; and

- Effective teachers are effective no matter what district they are in (Allington, 2009).

Language Arts/Literacy

On the following pages are lists of suggested interventions and how they may be appropriate for struggling students (Left Tiers 1, 2, 3) and for advanced students (Right Tiers 1, 2, 3). They are, by no means, complete lists. Still, they offer suggestions about how interventions may be approached so that no child is truly left behind. In this way, we can move toward insuring that all children can attain at least one year's growth for every year spent in school—surely the prime objective for all education.

Language Arts/Literacy Tier 1 Regular Classroom Setting With Differentiation

(Struggling)	(Advanced)
Universal classroom interventions targeted for support	Differentiated classroom challenges at challenge level
Leveled readers	Appropriate readers at above grade level
Variety of curriculum materials at appropriate level	Variety of curriculum materials at advanced level
Multiple resources at interest level and learning profiles	Multiple resources at advanced interest levels and learning profiles
Build background academic vocabulary knowledge	Extend and increase academic vocabulary knowledge
Small instructional groups at readiness level	Small instructional groups at readiness level
Use Bloom's Taxonomy for questioning using all levels	Use Bloom's Taxonomy for questioning using all levels BUT focusing on the higher levels
Focus on open-ended questions	Focus on open-ended questions using high level thinking and requiring documentation of answers
Use texts interesting to students around their passions at levels of reading difficulty	Use texts interesting to students around their passions at increased difficulty
Provide clearly written instructions in a step-by-step manner	Provide instructions giving clear parameters for completion with options for direction
Use multiple and flexible grouping activities	Use varied grouping opportunities including working with readiness peers and options for independent study
Adjust and expand time as needed	Condense standard curriculum time as much as possible, leaving more time to explore, experiment, and learn at an advanced level
Support from RtI specialists	Support from gifted education specialists
Focus on needs of struggling learners	Focus on needs of high-end learners including twice exceptional (2e) learners
Provide 8-10 repetitions for learning mastery; 17-25 repetitions may be necessary for some	Provide 1-5 repetitions for learning mastery
Determine prior knowledge before beginning unit	Determine prior knowledge to compact unit where possible
Present instruction using humor at appropriate pace for learners	Present instruction using humor at rapid pace
Stop often to summarize key elements in lesson	Stop occasionally to summarize key elements when necessary
Use cooperative groups of a mix of low to high-average students for progress	Use cooperative groups of high average to gifted mix of students for challenge

Language Arts/Literacy Tier 2 Core Instruction Plus Supplemental Instruction

Left (Struggling)	Right (Advanced)
K–1st daily 30-minute extra reading support plus RtI specialist support	30$^+$ minutes of advanced reading challenge and discussion, concept-based material
2nd $^+$ 60 minutes or more reading support with focus on comprehension and fluency	30-minute comparative book analysis and discussion with focus on high level reasoning skills (e.g. Junior Great Books)
Intervention groups of 1-1 to 1-3	Groups of 4-6 for discussion purposes
Address oral reading deficiencies	De-stress oral reading intensities; give opportunities for dramatic reading aloud
Focus on metacognition and comprehension in reading	Focus on making connections and conceptual understandings
Provide clearly written directions in a step-by-step manner	Provide limited directions leaving room for analysis and options
Use sequential instruction	Use instruction at high levels of depth and complexity
Use varied levels of Bloom's Taxonomy	Focus on higher levels of Bloom's Taxonomy
Use flexible grouping opportunities	Provide opportunities for high-end students to be together
Chunk learning opportunities in small chunks	Vary learning opportunities in larger chunks
Provide opportunities to grasp ideas	Provide opportunities to construct abstractions
Provide opportunities to understand meanings	Provide opportunities to draw inferences
Encourage satisfaction with learning	Ease self-criticism
Provide vocabulary at readiness level	Provide advanced vocabulary for challenge
Monitor student understanding so misunderstandings can be clarified	Monitor student mastery so advanced concepts can be presented

Language Arts/Literacy Tier 3 Intensive Interventions

Left (Struggling)	Right (Advanced)
Students show little progress in Tier 2	Students seldom challenged in Tier 2
Demonstrate significant struggles–need support	Twice exceptional (gifted and…)–need to address both exceptionalities
Intense tutorials	Need mentorships and independent study
Divide instruction into shorter segments	Present materials for greater depth and complexity at students' levels
Break assignments into smaller chunks	Increase pace (or slow down when material is extremely difficult or is of interest)
Use multi-sensory techniques for presentation of information	Provide opportunities to use and discuss intensities and overexcitabilities
Monitor student understandings and clarify misunderstandings	Provide high levels of intellectual challenge
Provide counseling and social skills instruction as needed	Provide advocacy for children who are significantly different from age peers
Address deficits in content areas	Provide opportunities for growth in areas of talent
Allow opportunities to be with students like themselves	Allow opportunities to be with students like themselves
Provide prompt/timely feedback to affirm efforts	Provide prompt/timely feedback to affirm efforts
Differentiate by content, process, product, and learning environment according to readiness, interests, and learning profiles	Differentiate by content, process, product, and learning environment according to readiness, interests, and learning profiles

A Scenario for Language Arts/Literacy

There are many possibilities for intervention for Right Tier students. Following is a possible scenario for a Right Tier book selection for Language Arts.

Recently, a teacher selected *Among the Hidden* by Margaret Haddix for study with eighth-grade middle-school advanced students. It is an excellent short novel that centers on a high level concept about the consequences of overpopulation. However, upon examination, it was discovered that this book, although excellent for discussion at a high conceptual level, had a very low readability level. There was little opportunity for vocabulary growth in high ability students at that grade level and limited discussion possibilities at an abstract level. The book is written for 8–12-year-olds (average) and would be more suitable for no more than fourth- or fifth-grade gifted students. (Note: Many advanced fourth graders will have already read books like the Harry Potter series by that time.) It could possibly be selected for a Tier 1 activity because of the readability level, but Right Tier 2 & 3 students would only benefit from a high level discussion with their academic peers.

On the other hand, *The Book Thief* by Markus Zusak is set during the Holocaust. It involves an illiterate girl who steals books from book-burnings as she develops a love of words and reading during the time of Nazi Germany. The book is superbly written, full of metaphor and rich language, and provides opportunities for high level discussion and deep thought. It is filled with German words. It also has some mild profanities that may concern some parents. Nevertheless, this is a perfect book study for Right Tier 2 and 3 students and has an acceptable reading level score such as determined by the Lexile Framework® for Reading or any other reading level measurement.

An excellent source for selection of appropriate reading for gifted and high average students is *Some of My Best Friends Are Books* 3rd Edition by Judith Wynn Halsted. It is divided into topics and grade levels and is an excellent resource for teachers and gifted education specialists.

Another way of approaching differentiation in Tier 1 and Right Tiers 2 and 3 is to focus on differentiating the type of questioning used in the classroom. One way is to use Socratic questioning. Socrates taught by asking questions which forced students to think at a deeper level. There are six types of questions (Paul & Elder, 2006):

- conceptual clarifications (*Why are you saying that?*);
- probing assumptions (*How can you verify or disprove that assumption?*);
- probing rationale, reasons, and evidence *(Can you give me an example of that?)*;
- questioning viewpoints and perspectives *(How could you look another way at this?)*;
- probing implications and consequences *(What are the consequences of that assumption?);* and
- questions about the question *(Why do you think I asked this question?)*.

A search on the Internet will provide more details for teachers. Another excellent source is Morgan and Saxton's excellent book *Asking Better Questions*.

Challenge in Math

Jennie Winters, Math & Science Coordinator; Lake CO ESC; Grayslake IL

Most of the research in RtI interventions has been in the area of literacy. We can learn much about the structure of interventions from the literacy world, as there are many commonalities between effective literacy instruction and effective mathematics instruction. For instance, effective instruction is at the students' developmental levels.

When examining intervention possibilities for mathematics, it is important to consider how literacy instruction and mathematics instruction differ. Literacy has one main goal, making meaning from text – better known as "comprehension." However, mathematics has multiple layers. The National Council for the Teachers of Mathematics (NCTM) has identified five content standards for mathematics and five process standards.

Content Standards

- Number Sense
- Algebra
- Geometry
- Measurement
- Data Analysis and Probability

Process Standards

- Problem Solving
- Reasoning and Proof
- Communication
- Connections
- Representation

Because mathematics has many entry points to understanding, we cannot assume students' levels unless we pre-assess their understanding in each of the content strands. Students who are strong in arithmetic may be weak in geometric reasoning. Students who are proficient at computation may be weak in problem solving. Therefore, instructional decisions based upon current student data are critical for meeting students' individual needs.

Once teachers have pre-assessment data, they can determine instructional pathways that are appropriate for students at their corresponding levels. Assessments that are open-ended will give teachers more information regarding student understanding than will selected-response tools–multiple choice, true/false, matching, and fill-in responses. Selected response assessments align well with knowledge and understanding targets, as well as with some patterns of reasoning (Stiggins, 2001). The best way to ascertain what students understand is to talk to them; however, it is challenging for teachers to interview each student regarding their understanding of each concept on a regular basis. Another way to uncover student understanding is to observe them manipulate both tools and information and to listen to students communicating with each other.

Much research has been done regarding the Concrete-Representational-Abstract (CRA) model of instruction for working with struggling learners, but it can also be applied to the needs of gifted learners (Witzel, Smith, & Brownell, 2001). This model consists of 3 phases:

1. Concrete Phase: Students are provided concrete manipulatives to make models of math concepts and to explore these concepts using both visual and tactile experiences.
2. Representational Phase: Students are encouraged to use visual models to represent concepts along with or instead of concrete manipulatives. The purpose is to allow students to step back from the concrete tools and explore the concepts or processes that the tools were used to model.
3. Abstract Phase: In this phase, students are able to work with mathematical concepts and processes without the aid of manipulatives or visual tools.

Interestingly, advanced learners are often introduced to concepts in the abstract phase because of their advanced status. However, if these learners are only introduced to the procedural understanding without the conceptual link, it is questionable as to how deeply they actually understand these concepts. Therefore, it is helpful to think of CRA as a continuum. If advanced learners can grasp the concepts when presented to them in an abstract format, they can be challenged to examine the concept more deeply by representing it with visual or concrete models. They can also be challenged to describe a context for their abstract understandings.

In mathematics instruction, advanced learners may be introduced to procedures and concepts at a more rapid pace than average or below average learners. This pacing can challenge them to absorb more advanced concepts, but it can also proceduralize the concepts to the point that they are not comprehending them but merely "doing" them. To avoid the heavy focus on procedural understanding, it is important for both teachers and students to have opportunities to create contexts that are meaningful and to encourage the exploration of relationships between concepts and procedures.

For example, consider the great push for Algebra for all in the United States. Algebra is the study of patterns, problem solving, procedures, and relationships. When students are asked to compute without a context, they may be using procedures to solve problems, but they may not be able to uncover patterns or relationships. The following pages describe differences between left and right components of math interventions for struggling and advanced students in Tiers 1, 2, and 3.

Tier 1 Regular Classroom Setting with Differentiation

(Struggling)	(Advanced)
Begin instruction in Concrete phase, move to Representational phase, and then to Abstract phase of instruction	Begin instruction in Abstract phase, but challenge students to create concrete and representational models that utilize the concept
Build background academic vocabulary knowledge	Extend and increase academic vocabulary knowledge
Focus on open-ended questions	Focus on open-ended questions using high level thinking and requiring documentation of answers
Provide clearly written instructions in a step-by-step manner, with concrete and visual models	Provide instructions giving clear parameters for completion with options for direction
Stop often to summarize key elements in the lesson	Stop occasionally to summarize key elements, and discuss the connections to previously learned skills and concepts when necessary
Use collaborative learning in problem-solving situations to foster connections, and give students opportunities to take risks with peer support	Use collaborative learning to foster connections, and give students opportunities to challenge each other's reasoning in problem solving situations

Tier 2 Core Instruction Plus Supplemental Instruction

Left (Struggling)	Right (Advanced)
K–1st daily 30-minute extra math support plus RtI specialist support	30^+ minutes advanced problem-solving, challenge, and discussion, concept-based material
2nd $^+$ 60 minutes or more conceptual understanding	30-minute problem-solving extension and application of concepts
Address math fact deficiencies	De-stress factual understanding and extend to the search for patterns and relationships
Focus on metacognition and conceptual understanding in a context of problem solving	Focus on making connections and conceptual understandings to apply to problem-solving situations
Provide clearly written directions and visual cues in a step-by-step manner that focus on linking procedures and concepts	Provide limited directions leaving room for analysis and extension of thinking into similar problem-solving scenarios
Use concrete and visual models for students to acquire concepts	Encourage students to create concrete, visual, and contextual models for developing deep understanding of abstract concepts

Tier 2 Core Instruction Plus Supplemental Instruction

Left (Struggling)	Right (Advanced)
Break concepts into smaller chunks of understanding, and provide explicit instruction to connect these chunks so that the concept becomes clear	Vary learning opportunities in larger chunks
Provide opportunities to grasp ideas	Provide opportunities to construct abstractions
Provide opportunities for students to model possible solutions when problems have multiple possibilities for solutions	Provide opportunities to create knowledge with open-ended problems or problems with multiple solutions
Pre-teach both concrete and abstract vocabulary at the readiness level prior to classroom instruction, using concrete or visual models and practical contexts	Provide opportunities for students to acquire advanced vocabulary as well as create multiple contexts for appropriate usage of mathematics terminology
Monitor student understanding so misunderstandings can be clarified, and destroy misconceptions by demonstrating with models and simulations	Monitor student mastery so advanced and/or abstract concepts can be presented, and students can both apply and create knowledge in problem-solving situations

Tier 3 Intensive Interventions using CRA

Left (Struggling)	Right (Advanced)
Model concepts with unique manipulative tools to provide experience with multiple ways of representing concepts	Provide students opportunities to create unique representations of concepts and devise their own manipulatives and visuals
Provide more time for students to practice math skills and reinforce math concepts	Provide more time for students to expand and explain their thinking in problem-solving situations
Provide further opportunities for students to explain their thinking both verbally and with models	Ask students to create proof, pictures, and diagrams for abstract concepts
Assess student understanding of concepts through scaffolded questioning	Assess students' depth of understanding of math concepts and skills through probative questioning from both teacher and peers

Differentiated Questioning

"Posing questions is the central act of reading the world: it must become a habit. I wish I could give you a handy kitbag of reliable questions to try, but there can be no prescribable set of sure fire questions. The whole game is one giant improvisation . . . the questions themselves are far less important than the habit of questioning." (Booth, 1999, p. 210)

Norah Morgan and Juliana Saxton (2006) discuss two main factors for teachers to consider when designing questions:
1. What kind of thinking is the question generating?
2. How will this question help engage my students with the material?

If we want advanced mathematics learners to deepen their understanding, we need to design questions that are more than just open-ended. They must push students to consider multiple possibilities. They must cause students to create understanding of ideas rather than just do math.

Morgan and Saxton (2006) also discuss the levels of questioning in Bloom's Taxonomy. Following are example math questions for each of the levels.

Remembering (Knowledge)	If each side is 2 toothpicks, how many toothpicks are required to make the square?
Understanding (Comprehension)	How many more toothpicks will it take to make a square with sides of 3 than a triangle with sides of 3?
Solving (Application)	How would you determine the side of a triangle using 15 total toothpicks?
Reasoning (Analysis)	Why is it beneficial to determine the rule for n sides of the triangle and square?

**Creating
(Synthesis)**   How can you develop a table and rule to represent the toothpicks needed for forming hexagons?

**Judging
(Evaluation)**   What is the most important piece of information you need in predicting the length of sizes of an unknown shape?
What is the benefit of making a table?

Example starters for probing questions could include:

What if . . .?   What other way . . .?
How would you compare . . .?   How would you portray . . .?
Would you agree that . . .?   Would you describe what happened when . . .?

Teachers who want to stretch students' thinking make a paradigm shift from:

- Thinking "What type of question should I ask?";
- Using a step-by-step method that follows a framework; and
- Asking many questions that focus on answers.

Moving toward:

- Thinking "What do I want this question to do?";
- Using strategic questioning based on student thinking; and
- Asking fewer questions by choosing ones that focus on thinking.

An interesting dilemma occurs when teachers work with students who have processing deficits but high intellectual capabilities:

The Case of Nathan–The LD/Gifted Student

Nathan was a student whose IQ was extremely high, but he was diagnosed with visual and auditory processing difficulties. Nathan's learning disability and high intellectual abilities were not identified until he reached fourth grade. Until that time, some teachers misinterpreted Nathan's behaviors as a lack of motivation. Others thought he was a "slow learner." He often struggled in math, yet he could memorize facts and procedures with minimum support. His major challenges were with problem-solving situations and developing a deep understanding of math concepts. The textbook Nathan was using was on the traditional end of the spectrum–more focused on practicing procedures than on problem solving. Some expected Nathan to thrive with such a tool, but he was bored and unmotivated. Nathan expressed his frustrations by refusing to work. In whole group problem-solving situations, Nathan would contribute his thoughts, but he refused to complete problem-solving assignments independently.

Nathan was used to computing accurately when given number sentences because he could apply the memorized procedures and facts to those tasks. However, processing the more abstract situations was challenging. He lacked strategies for organizing and analyzing the information when given a situation or context.

Nathan needed challenge, but he also needed explicit instruction in strategic thinking. Through careful questioning and the use of visual models, teachers could guide Nathan to attempt problem-solving situations more independently. They used a combination of abstract and concrete instruction to support his unique needs.

The interventions stated within this chapter provide a Response to Intelligence that accommodates ALL students. With the RtI initiative, we must assure that our entire student population will have the opportunity to learn at a level that will provide struggle and challenge for their academic growth. Every student has the right to grow at least one year for every year spent in school–including the gifted student.

Our best resources are reading, math, RtI, and gifted education specialists in each school district. There are also excellent reading lists through organizational websites such as http://www.hoagiesgifted.org and from local public libraries.

"All children deserve the right to learn at their highest level of readiness . . . even the gifted."

Bertie Kingore

REFERENCES

Allington, R. L. (2009). *What really matters in response to intervention: Research-based designs.* Boston, MA: Pearson.

Booth, E. (1999). *The everyday work of art.* Lincoln, NE: iUniverse.com

Morgan, N., & Saxton, J. (2006). *Asking better questions* (2nd ed.). Markham, Ontario, Canada: Pembroke.

Paul, R. & Elder, L. (2006). *The thinker's guide to the art of Socratic questioning.* Dillon Beach, CA: The Foundation for Critical Thinking.

Stiggins, R. J. (2001). *Student-involved classroom assessment.* Upper Saddle River, NJ: Merrill Prentice Hall.

Witzel, B., Smith, S. W., & Brownell, M. T. (2001). How can I help students with learning disabilities in algebra? *Intervention in School and Clinic, 37,* 101–104.

Chapter 8

The End and a Beginning

Every child enters school for the first time excited about the opportunity to learn. But, far too many languish in the classroom. It is not uncommon for these children to learn that school is very easy. School can become boring as children sit in their seats having to repeat work they have already mastered. Repeatedly they are forced to complete unchallenging material. Many even ultimately learn that school is *not* the place to go for learning. Real learning takes place for these students outside the brick and mortar school. Some gifted and talented children sit quietly in their classrooms, perhaps daydreaming about their personal areas of passion. Some become behavior problems. Some drop out of school as soon as they can.

These students can spend up to six hours a day waiting to learn something new. Talents and gifts are squandered, and many students learn the message that they don't have to work, risk, and struggle because they "get by" without challenge. They may even come to think that this is what school is about. How many of us know someone who cruised through school never having to do a bit of work, yet still receiving good grades? Students who learn this message are at a disadvantage because somewhere in their lives–high school, college, or beyond–they come up against a challenge and don't know how to handle it. Some may even "crash and burn."

Stories of these children are everywhere. Examples occur in Jan and Bob Davidson's (2004) powerful book, *Genius Denied: How to Stop Wasting Our Brightest Young Minds*. Research documents that this situation happens too often. In the research report *A Nation Deceived: How Schools Hold Back America's Brightest Students* (Colangelo, Assouline, & Gross, 2004), documentation of how the gifted fall through the cracks is clear. The National Research Center on the Gifted and Talented (NRC/GT) through funding from the Jacob K. Javits Gifted and Talented Students Education Act has published extensive evidence of this sad fact for years.

But there is hope. Recognition of the need for change is beginning to happen. Professional journals are focusing on addressing the needs of gifted and talented children through RtI. In 2009, an entire professional journal of gifted education was devoted to meeting the needs of these children. One article, *RtI Models for Gifted Children* (Rollins, Mursky, Shah-Coultrane, & Johnsen, 2009) suggests models that are used in a few states. It describes an excellent assessment tool for looking at a school's RtI model in providing for gifted students. *Designing Services and Programs for High-Ability Learners: A Guidebook for Gifted Education* (Purcell, & Eckert, 2006) presents chapters that address the specific need for services for these children. Written by some of the most respected experts in the field, chapters include suggestions for curriculum, services that meet the social and emotional needs of gifted children, and how to align gifted education services with general education.

But change happens slowly. Until change takes place in schools, gifted and talented children are being lost in an educational system that focuses on minimum competency–a measure that documents the least a child needs to get by–through high-stakes testing. Response to Intervention continues this trend by focusing on struggling learners and grade-level curriculum.

Differentiation is assumed to be taking place in the regular classroom, yet research study after research study confirms that differentiation seldom takes place (Reis, et al., 1993). Teachers are given classrooms that are increasing in size, and the differences and needs among students are widening and are becoming more diverse. Small wonder teachers are stressed.

But can we afford to lose this precious resource by leaving gifted children to fend for themselves in classrooms? These children are the forgotten children in education. Common misconceptions and myths about them continue to thrive. People continue to believe that these children can make it on their own–that they don't need help or opportunities to struggle with new material, and receive encouragement and support for doing so. A truly gifted child is not necessarily excellent in everything–every content area and every skill level. This assumes that the gifted are like Mary Poppins, "perfect in every way."

The truth is that gifted children come in all packages, talents, and abilities, in all colors, shapes, and sizes. Many can be called or are underachievers.

Many carry a double label, "gifted and . . ." (learning disabled, second language learners, behavior problems, etc.). Many go unrecognized in a school system that neither understands nor nourishes their needs. But students have rights, too.

Rights of Students

Carol J. Morreale (1993) states:

ALL Students need and deserve an equal opportunity:

. . . to stretch their minds around new and difficult curriculum, content, maximize their potential, and demand the use of higher level thinking. Differentiation within classrooms is important. Gifted students need teachers who can and will modify the standard curriculum to make it more intellectually demanding. Gifted students particularly need a quicker pace, a greater depth, and more abstract processes. All students need a level of content slightly beyond their grasp, so they will apply higher level thinking.

. . . to learn how to learn, which requires organizational skills, study skills, and persistence. For gifted students, this occurs only when curriculum is challenging and they are held accountable.

. . . to feel part of a group and to learn together with intellectual peers for at least part of every school day. Gifted students need to feel connected with age mates and also with other gifted students. Learning with others of similar ability makes them feel less isolated and more stimulated.

. . . to have their abilities recognized and challenges early. Any exceptionality requires early intervention to develop full potential. In the primary grades, academic rigor is as important as socialization skills. Without appropriate academic challenge for young children, educators may unknowingly ask children to deny who they are.

. . . to develop their uniqueness in a psychologically nurturing environment. Gifted students sense that their peers are impatient with the depth of their questions, the sophistication of their vocabulary, and the uniqueness of their interests. They need significant adults in their world to accept and assist with social/emotional issues that relate to self-understanding, peer relations, and family relations.

. . . to be fully engaged in the learning process. Because gifted students often come to class with a broad knowledge base, they spend a great deal of time waiting to learn something new. Professional development and stronger teacher certification requirements are needed for staff to be able to provide appropriate educational experiences that will engage gifted students.

. . . to be free from discrimination based on intellect, gender, race, poverty, or age. Meeting the needs of the gifted should not depend on the community one lives in or traditional role expectations. For example, gifted students may need earlier access to school or curriculum levels. Gifted females may need encouragement to pursue accelerated math and /or science classes. Students in low socio-economic areas should have equal access to gifted programming based on local standards.

. . . to experience the joy of learning and succeeding, feeling which is contagious and has life-long positive effects.

You have a right . . .

1. . . . to know about your giftedness.

2. . . . to learn something new every day.

3. . . . to be passionate about your talent area without apologies.

4. . . . to have an identity beyond your talent area.

5. . . . to feel good about your accomplishments.

6. . . . to make mistakes.

7. . . . to seek guidance in the development of your talent.

8. . . . to have multiple peer groups and a variety of friends.

9. . . . to choose which of your talent areas you wish to pursue.

10. . . . not to be gifted at everything.

Del Siegle, 2007–2009 NAGC President

NAGC has published a list of rights for gifted children and is available through their website (http://www.nagc.org)

Turn RtI into a true and priceless diamond of education, providing appropriate challenge and struggle for each and every child placed in our care–including the thousands of gifted and talented children in classrooms everywhere.

Then we will truly demonstrate a **"Response to Intelligence."**

REFERENCES

Colangelo, N., Assouline, S. G., & Gross, M. (2004). *A nation deceived: How schools hold back America's brightest students.* Iowa City: The University of Iowa, The Connie Belin & Jacqueline N. Blank International Center for Gifted Education and Talent Development.

Davidson, J., & Davidson, B. (with L. Vanderkam). (2004). *Genius denied: How to stop wasting our brightest young minds.* New York, NY: Simon & Schuster.

Purcell, J. H., & Eckert, R. D. (Eds.). (2006). *Designing services and programs for high-ability learners: A guidebook for gifted education.* Thousand Oaks, CA: Corwin Press.

Reis, S. M., Westberg, K. L., Kulikowich, J., Caillard, F., Hébert, T., Plucker, J., . . . Smist, J. M. (1993). *Why not let high ability students start school in January? The curriculum compacting study* (Research Monograph 93106). Storrs: University of Connecticut, The National Research Center on the Gifted and Talented.

Rollins, K., Mursky, C. V., Shah-Coltrane, S., & Johnsen, S. K. (2009). RtI models for gifted children. *Gifted Child Today, 32*(3), 21–30.

Terms

ADD - Attention-Deficit Disorder

ADHD – Attention-Deficit Hyperactivity Disorder

ARRA – American Recovery and Reinvestment Act

Acceleration – an intervention that increases the rate at which students learn skills and concepts; moving ahead grade levels

Advocacy – active verbal support for a cause or position

Affective differentiation – learning experiences based on social-emotional needs of gifted children through counseling and support at different times according to their needs

Asperger's syndrome – an autism spectrum disorder that is characterized by significant difficulties in social interaction, social isolation, eccentric behavior, and restricted and repetitive patterns of behavior and interests

Asynchronistic – uneven development that is out of sync with age peers

Behavioral learner – learner who needs to dig in and learn by experiencing

Brainstorming – generating creative ideas spontaneously, usually for problem-solving, and especially in an intensive group discussion that does not allow time for reflection

CEC-TAG – Council for Exceptional Children – Talented and Gifted

Cluster grouping – placing high-ability students in a small group with teacher facilitation and performing higher level work

Code-switching – able to switch between two (or more) languages using elements of both and following correct grammatical rules.

Compacting – first identifying the learning objectives that need to be mastered. Assessments are then offered to those who think they already know the material. Based on the successful assessment results, students may be offered curriculum extensions in order to avoid repetition or review of mastered material.

Cooperative learning groups – small groups whose purpose is to develop peer interaction and cooperation while working on an assignment

Creativity – the ability to use the imagination to develop new and original ideas or things involving fluency, flexibility, originality, and elaboration

Differentiation – the adaptation and modification of age-appropriate learning experiences in order to address the differences in student readiness levels, interests, and learning profiles

Enrichment – to improve the quality and depth of learning of a topic, usually by adding in-depth activities

Evidence-based instruction – instruction that is based on empirical research methods and has been accepted and/or approved by experts in the field after rigorous review

Figural learner – learner who needs to touch or manipulate in order to learn about the topic

Flexible grouping – students make constant changes in grouping depending on needs

Higher order thinking skills – activities that are based on critical and creative thinking skills at the higher levels; i.e. analysis, synthesis, evaluation of Bloom's Taxonomy

IDEA – Individuals with Disabilities Education Act

Intervention – a strategy implemented in order to improve a student's performance and/or need

Lexile score – a common scale for matching reader ability and text difficulty based on comprehension

Mentoring – relationship in which a more experienced or more knowledgeable person helps a less experienced or less knowledgeable person in a content area

Minimum competency – a measure that documents the least a child needs to "get by" or pass the high-stakes test

NAGC – National Association for Gifted Children

NCLB – No Child Left Behind Act

Problem-based learning – student-centered instructional teaching strategy in which students collaboratively solve problems and reflect on their experiences; challenges students to learn to learn

Progress monitoring – on-going assessment to determine curriculum strengths, weaknesses, and achievement that leads to identification and effectiveness of intervention strategies and needs of students

Race to the Top – part of the American Recovery and Reinvestment Act of 2009; a competitive grant program designed to encourage and reward states that create conditions for education innovation and reform

R.A.F.T. activities – a differentiation strategy using a framework for approaching writing that can be especially good for encouraging expressions of empathy and understanding of another perspective. R = role; A = audience; F – format; T = topic

Replacement class – grouping of students for reading, math, or other subjects for full daily instruction from a specialist who uses compacting, acceleration, and enrichment of the curriculum in order to meet students' needs

Resident expert – students who know the subject well – know as much, if not more than the text

Response to Intelligence – the recognition of and commitment to providing academic challenge and social/emotional support to children of high potential understanding that all children, including the gifted, have the right to grow at least one year for every year spent in school so they are prepared to thrive in the 21st century

RtI – Response to Intervention; Response to Instruction; Response to Intelligence

Scaffolding – a structure of supports such as tutors or introductory tools to build on what the student knows so that he/she may experience success and growth

Scatter score – discrepancy scores on subtests of IQ measures that may indicate identification of the twice exceptional gifted child

Semantic learner – learner who excels through words

Symbolic learner – learner who is facile with numbers, phonics, and symbols

Telescoping – instruction that takes less time than normal (e.g. a one-year course in one semester or three years of middle school in two years)

Tier 1 – scientific-based instruction for all students, differentiated where necessary

Tier 2 – small group intervention using scientific-based strategies for those not achieving skills presented in Tier 1

Tier 3 – one-on-one or small groups for those who need more individualized instruction than Tier 2 with intensive interventions to improve and support skills

Tiering – either curriculum and instruction-varied levels of the required curriculum in order to meet the needs of students where they are

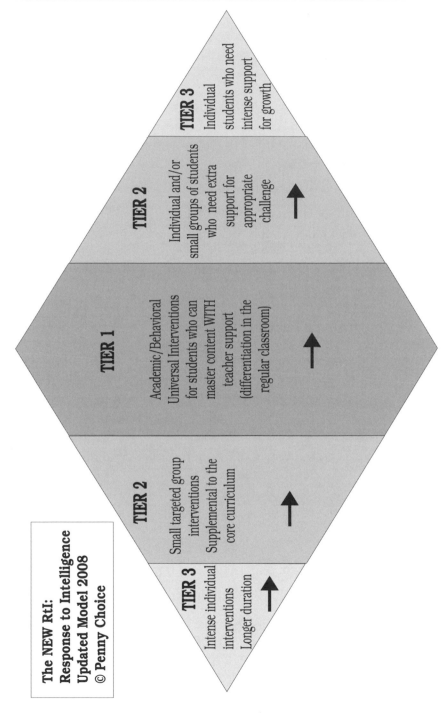

The NEW RtI:
Response to Intelligence
Updated Model 2008
© Penny Choice

TIER 3
Intense individual
interventions
Longer duration

TIER 2
Small targeted group
interventions
Supplemental to the
core curriculum

TIER 1
Academic/Behavioral
Universal Interventions
for students who can
master content WITH
teacher support
(differentiation in the
regular classroom)

TIER 2
Individual and/or
small groups of students
who need extra
support for
appropriate
challenge

TIER 3
Individual
students who need
intense support
for growth

Objective for struggling students: To be successful at Tier 1 or higher.

Objective for advanced students: To receive appropriate challenge for growth (and skill development) at least 1 year for every year spent in school.

Resources

Archambault, F. A., Jr., Westberg, K. L., Brown, S. W., Hallmark, B. W., Emmons, C. L., & Zhang, W. (1993). *Regular classroom practices with gifted students: Results of a national survey of classroom teachers* (Research Monograph 93102). Storrs: University of Connecticut, The National Research Center on the Gifted and Talented.

Baldwin, A. (1985b). *Baldwin identification matrix 2*. New York, NY: Trillium.

Benson, B. (2003). *Differentiated instructional strategies for writing in the content areas*. Thousand Oaks, CA: Corwin Press.

Betts, G. T. (2000). *Curriculum differentiation & revised learner model*. Washington, DC: National Association for Gifted Children.

Bloom, B. (Ed.). (1956). *Taxonomy of educational objectives: Handbook I. Cognitive domain*. New York, NY: McKay.

Burns, D. (2000). *The differentiation dilemma*. Washington, DC: National Association for Gifted Children.

Burns, D., & Purcell, J. (2001). *A framework for providing a differentiated grades 4–6 reading curriculum*. Washington, DC: National Association for Gifted Children.

Chapman, C., & King, R. (2003). *Differentiated instructional strategies for reading in the content areas*. Thousand Oaks, CA: Corwin Press.

Chapman, C., & King, R. (2005). *Differentiated assessment strategies: One tool doesn't fit all*. Thousand Oaks, CA: Corwin Press.

Clark, B. (2008). *Growing up gifted: Developing the potential of children at home and at school* (7th ed.). Upper Saddle River, NJ: Pearson.

Coil, C. (2004). *Activities and assessments for the differentiated classroom*. Marion, IL: Pieces of Learning.

Coil, C. (2007). *Successful teaching in the differentiated classroom*. Marion, IL: Pieces of Learning.

Coil, C., (2009). *Differentiation, RTI, and achievement: How they work together*. Marion, IL: Pieces of Learning.

Colangelo, N., Assouline, S., & Gross, M. (2004). *A nation deceived: How schools hold back America's brightest students* (Vols. 1 & 2). Iowa City: The University of Iowa, The Connie Belin & Jacqueline N. Blank International Center for Gifted Education and Talent Development.

Coleman, M. R. (2003). *The identification of students who are gifted* (ERIC Digest #ED480431). Arlington, VA: The ERIC Clearing House. Retrieved from http://www.eric.ed.gov/ERICWebPortal/search.

Conover, L. (2001). *Middle school environments that support differentiated instruction*. Washington, DC: National Association for Gifted Children.

Daniels, S., & Piechowski, M. M. (Eds.). (2009). *Living with intensity: Understanding the sensitivity, excitability, and emotional development of gifted children, adolescents, and adults*. Scottsdale, AZ: Great Potential Press.

Davidson, K., & Decker, T. (2006). *Bloom's and beyond: Higher level questions & activities for the creative classroom*. Marion, IL: Pieces of Learning.

Davies, G. (1983). *Practical primary drama*. London, England: Heinemann.

Davis, G. A., & Rimm, S. B. (2003). *Education of the gifted and talented* (5th ed.). Boston, MA: Allyn and Bacon.

Delisle, J., & Galbraith, J. (2002). *When gifted kids don't have all the answers*. Minneapolis, MN: Free Spirit.

Duffett, A., Farkas, S., & Loveless, T. (2008). *High achieving students in the era of NCLB*. Washington, D.C.: Thomas B. Fordham Institute.

Eidson, C., Iseminger, R., & Taibbi, C. (2007). *Demystifying differentiation in middle school*. Marion, IL: Pieces of Learning.

Eidson, C,, Iseminger, R., & Taibbi, C. (2008). *Demystifying differentiation in elementary school*. Marion, IL: Pieces of Learning.

Erickson, L. (2002). *Concept-based curriculum*. Thousand Oaks, CA: Corwin Press.

Ford, D. (2004b). *Intelligence testing and cultural diversity: Concerns, cautions, and considerations* (Research Monograph 04204). Storrs, CT: University of Connecticut, National Research Center on the Gifted and Talented.

Frischknecht, J., & Schroeder, E. (2006). *Asking smart questions*. Marion, IL: Pieces of Learning.

Gardner, H. (1999). *Intelligence reframed: Multiple intelligences for the 21st century*. New York, NY: Basic Books.

Gregory, G., & Chapman, C. (2002). *Differentiated instructional strategies: One size doesn't fit all*. Thousand Oaks, CA: Corwin Press.

Gregory, G., & Chapman, C. (2008). *Activities for the differentiated classroom: Grades 6-8 science*. Thousand Oaks, CA: Corwin Press.

Fayer, L., & Walker, S. (2009). *Constructing curriculum units using backward design*. Marion, IL: Pieces of Learning.

Haddix, M.P. (1998). *Among the hidden*. New York, NY: Simon & Schuster.

Halsted, J.W. (2009). *Some of my best friends are books: Guiding gifted readers from preschool to high school* (3rd ed.). Scottsdale, AZ: Great Potential Press.

Heacox, D. (2002). *Differentiating instruction in the regular classroom*. Minneapolis, MN: Free Spirit.

Heacox, D. (2009). *Making differentiation a habit: How to ensure success in academically diverse classrooms*. Minneapolis, MN: Free Spirit.

Heathcote, D., & Bolton, G. (1995). *Drama for learning*. Portsmouth, NH: Heinemann.

Hébert, T. P., Cramond, B. L, Millar, G., & Silvian, A. F. (2002). *E. Paul Torrance: His life, accomplishments, and legacy* (Research Monograph No. 02152). Storrs: University of Connecticut, The National Research Center on the Gifted and Talented.

Kaplan, S., & Cannon, M.W. (2000). *Curriculum starter cards: Developing differentiated lessons for gifted students.* Austin, TX: Texas Association for the Gifted and Talented.

Karnes, F. A., & Bean, S.M. (2007). *Methods and materials for teaching the gifted* (3rd ed.). Waco, TX: Prufrock Press.

Kerr, B. (1994). *Smart girls two: A new psychology of girls, women, and giftedness.* Scottsdale, AZ: Great Potential Press.

Kerr, B. (2001). *Smart boys: Talent, manhood, and the search for meaning.* Scottsdale, AZ: Great Potential Press.

Kingore, B. (2004). *Differentiation: Simplified, realistic and effective: How to challenge advanced potentials in mixed-ability classrooms.* Austin, TX: Professional Associates Publishing.

Kitano, M. K., & Espinosa, R. (1995). Language diversity and giftedness: Working with gifted English language learners. *Journal for the Education of the Gifted, 18,* 234-254.

Kitano, M., Montgomery, D., VanTassel-Baska, J., Johnsen, Susan., (2008). *Using the national gifted education standards.* National Association for Gifted Children and the Council for Exceptional Children-The Association for the Gifted. Thousand Oaks, CA: Corwin Press.

Logan, K. S., Rizza, M. G., Gubbins, E. J., Gavin, M. K., Kloosterman, V. I., Schuler, P. A., . . . Suroviak, C. E. (1997). *A compendium of research-based information on the education of gifted and talented students.* Storrs: University of Connecticut, The National Research Center on the Gifted and Talented.

Lovecky, D.V. (2004). *Different minds: Gifted children with AD/HD, Asperger syndrome, and other learning deficits*. London, England: Jessica Kingsley.

Lujan, M.L., Collins, B., & Love, S. (2009). *Response to intervention (RtI) strategies*. Tyler, TX: Mentoring Minds.

Marland, S. P., Jr. (1972). *Education of the gifted and talented: Report to the Congress of the United States by the U.S. Commissioner of Education and background papers submitted to the U.S. Office of Education*. Washington, DC: U.S. Government Printing Office. (Government Documents Y4.L 11/2: G36)

National Commission on Excellence in Education. (1983). *A nation at risk: The imperative for educational reform*. Washington, DC: U.S. Government Printing Office.

Neelands, J. (1984). *Making sense of drama: A guide to classroom practice*. London, England: Heinemann.

O'Neill C. (1995). *Drama worlds: A framework for process drama*. Portsmouth, NH: Heinemann.

O'Neill, C., & Lambert, A. (1982). *Drama structures*. London, England: Hutchinson.

Piechowski, M.M. (2006). "Mellow out," they say. If I only could: *Intensities and sensitivities of the young and bright*. Madison, WI: Yunasa.

Piirto, J. (2004). *Understanding creativity*. Scottsdale, AZ: Great Potential Press.

Plucker, J.A., & Callahan, C.M. (2008). *Critical issues and practices in gifted education: What the research says*. Waco, TX: Prufrock Press.

Reis, S.M., Burns, D.E., & Renzulli, J. (1992). *Curriculum compacting: The complete guide to modifying the regular curriculum for high ability students*. Mansfield Center, CT: Creative Learning Press.

Roberts, J.L., & Inman, T.F. (2008). *Strategies for differentiating instruction: Best practices for the classroom* (2nd Ed.). Waco, TX: Prufrock Press.

Robinson, A., Shore, B. M., & Enersen, D.L. (2007). *Best practices in gifted education: An evidence-based guide.* Waco, TX: Prufrock Press.

Rogers, K. (2002). Re-forming Gifted Education. Scottsdale AZ: Great Potential Press.

Siegle, D. (2004). *Using media and technology with gifted learners.* Waco, TX: Prufrock Press.

Silverman, L. (1997) The construct of asynchronous development. *Peabody Journal of Education, 72*(3&4), 36-58.

Smutny, J., Walker, S., & Meckstroth, E. (1997). *Teaching young gifted children in the regular classroom: Identifying, nurturing, and challenging ages 4–9.* Minneapolis, MN: Free Spirit.

Strickland, C. (2007). *Tools for high-quality differentiated instruction.* Alexandria, VA: Association for Supervision and Curriculum Development.

Swartz, L. (1988). *Dramathemes.* Markham, Ontario, Canada: Pembroke.

Tomlinson, C. A. (1999). *The differentiated classroom: Responding to the needs of all learners.* Alexandria, VA: Association for Supervision and Curriculum Development.

Tomlinson, C.A. (2001). *How to differentiate instruction in mixed-ability classrooms* (2nd ed.). Alexandria, VA: Association for Supervision and Curriculum Development.

Tomlinson, C.A. (2003). *Differentiation in practice: A resource guide for differentiating curriculum grades 5–9.* Alexandria, VA: Association for Supervision and Curriculum Development.

Tomlinson, C.A. (2003). *Fulfilling the promise of the differentiated classroom: Strategies and tools for responsive teaching.* Alexandria, VA: Association for Supervision and Curriculum Development.

Tomlinson, C.A. (2004). *Differentiation for gifted and talented students.* Thousand Oaks, CA: Corwin Press.

Tomlinson, C. (2005). Quality curriculum and instruction for highly able students. *Theory Into Practice, 44,* 160–166.

Tomlinson, C. A. (2008). *Differentiated education.* In J. A. Plucker & C. M. Callahan (Eds.), *Critical issues and practices in gifted education: What the research says* (pp. 167–177). Waco, TX: Prufrock Press

Tomlinson, C.A., & Allen, S.D. (2000). *Leadership for differentiating schools & classrooms.* Alexandria, VA: Association for Supervision and Curriculum Development.

Tomlinson, C.A., & Cunningham-Eidson, C. (2003). *Differentiation in practice: A resource guide for differentiating curriculum grades K–5.* Alexandria, VA: Association for Supervision and Curriculum Development.

Tomlinson, C.A., & McTighe, J. (2006). *Integrating differentiated instruction & understanding by design: Connecting content and kids.* Alexandria, VA: Association for Supervision and Curriculum Development.

Tomlinson, C.A., & Strickland, C.A. (2005). *Differentiation in practice: A resource guide for differentiating curriculum grades 9–12.* Alexandria, VA: Association for Supervision and Curriculum Development.

Tomlinson, C.A., & Narvaez, L. (2008). *The differentiated school: Making revolutionary changes in teaching and learning.* Alexandria, VA: Association for Supervision and Curriculum Development.

VanTassel-Baska, J. (2003). *Curriculum planning and instructional design for gifted learners.* Denver, CO: Love.

VanTassel-Baska, J., & Brown, E. (2009). An analysis of gifted education curricular models. In F. A. Karnes & S. M. Bean (Eds.), *Methods and materials for teaching the gifted* (3rd ed.). Waco, TX: Prufrock Press.

VanTassel-Baska, J., Feldhusen, J., Seeley, K., Wheatley, G., Silverman, L., & Foster, W. (1988). *Comprehensive curriculum for gifted learners*. Needham Heights, MA: Allyn and Bacon.

VanTassel-Baska, J., & Little, C. A. (Eds.). (2003). *Content-based curriculum for high-ability learners*. Waco, TX: Prufrock Press.

VanTassel-Baska, J., & Stambaugh, T. (2007). *Overlooked GEMS: A national perspective on low-income promising learners*. Washington, DC: National Association for Gifted Children.

VanTassel-Baska, J., Zuo, L., Avery, L. D., & Little, C. A. (2002). A curriculum study of gifted student learning in the language arts. *Gifted Child Quarterly, 46*, 30–44.

Wagner, B. J. (1998). *Educational drama and language arts: What research shows*. Portsmouth, NH: Heinemann.

Walker, S. Y. (2002). *The survival guide for parents of gifted kids*. Minneapolis, MN: Free Spirit.

Webb, J., Meckstroth, E., & Tolan, S. (1989). *Guiding the gifted child*. Scottsdale, AZ: Gifted Psychology Press.

Weinfeld, R., Barnes-Robins, L., Jeweler, S., & Roffman Shevitz, B. (2006). *Smart kids with learning difficulties: Overcoming obstacles and realizing potential*. Waco, TX: Prufrock Press.

Wilhelm, J.D., & Edmiston, B. (1998). *Imagining to learn: Inquiry, ethics, and integration through drama*. Portsmouth, NH: Heinemann.

Winebrenner, S. (2001). *Teaching gifted kids in the regular classroom*. Minneapolis, MN: Free Spirit.

Winebrenner, S. (2005). *Differentiating content for gifted learners in grades 6–12*. Minneapolis, MN: Free Spirit.

Wormeli, R. (2006). *Fair isn't always equal: Assessing & grading in the differentiated classroom*. Portland, ME: Stenhouse.

Wormeli, R. (2007). *Differentiation: From planning to practice, grades 6–12*. Portland, ME: Stenhouse.

Zusak, M. (2005). *The book thief*. New York, NY: Knopf.

Index

The Authors

Penny Choice, M.A., M.Ed., is a consultant and retired Staff Development Coordinator for the Regional Office of Education, Grayslake, IL. She is a specialist in Gifted Education, differentiation and problem-based learning, curriculum and staff development, the Visual-Spatial Learner, process learning, and fine arts education with a focus in integrating the arts and the use of process drama. Penny is adjunct professor with Northeastern Illinois University, Chicago. She is Past Chair of the Arts Division and Past Chair of the Global Awareness Network for the National Association for Gifted Children and serves as Co-Chair for the Diverse Gifted Populations Committee for the Illinois Association for Gifted Children.

Sally Yahnke Walker, Ph.D., is a consultant and an advocate for gifted children. She is the Executive Director for the Illinois Association for Gifted Children. Sally has piloted programs to create a broad-based level of support for talented students in public school districts, provided in-service training for teachers, and facilitated workshops for parents of gifted children. Sally's background includes classroom teacher, Chairman of the Illinois State Advisory Board on Gifted and Talented, member of the Illinois State Advisory Committee for the Gifted Education Seminar, former Chairman of the State Task Force on Early Identification and Intervention of Young Gifted, and author.

Both can be scheduled for professional development through Pieces of Learning
800-729-5137 emily@piecesoflearning.com
www.creativelearningconsultants.com

The NEW RtI: Response to Intelligence by Penny Choice and Dr. Sally Walker is a highly innovative solution to the ongoing problem of how to educate the most underachieving student in American classrooms today—the gifted child. Like so many government initiatives before it, "Response to Intervention" (RtI) aims to close the achievement gap and ensure appropriate education for all students. However, as this book persuasively demonstrates, for the over 3 million highly able students attending schools in this country, RtI fails to stop the continued squandering of their talent and ability. Most significant for classroom teachers is the book's inclusive and very ingenious model—*Response to Intelligence*—which expands organically from RtI's design and extends its reach to students on *both* ends of the ability spectrum. The usefulness of this model becomes vividly clear through the authors' succinct instructions, as well as the many wonderful examples and visual aids they provide to help teachers respond to the unique needs of the gifted learners in their classrooms.

– Joan Smutny, Director, Center for Gifted, National-Louis University